hamlyn
Quick**Cook**

hamlyn
QuickCook
Low Fat

Recipes by Jo McAuley

Every dish, three ways – you choose!
30 minutes | 20 minutes | 10 minutes

An Hachette UK company
www.hachette.co.uk

First published in Great Britain in 2012 by Hamlyn,
a division of Octopus Publishing Group Ltd
Endeavour House, 189 Shaftesbury Avenue, London WC2H 8JY
www.octopusbooks.co.uk

Recipes by Jo McAuley
Copyright © Octopus Publishing Group Ltd 2012

ISBN: 978-0-60062-368-7

A CIP catalogue record for this book is available from the British Library

Printed and bound in China

1 2 3 4 5 6 7 8 9 10

Both metric and imperial measurements are given for the recipes. Use one set of
measurements only, not a mixture of both.

Standard level spoon measurements are used in all recipes
1 tablespoon = 15 ml
1 teaspoon = 5 ml

Ovens should be preheated to the specified temperature. If using a fan-assisted
oven, follow the manufacturer's instructions for adjusting the time and temperature.

Eggs should be medium unless otherwise stated. The Department of Health advises
that eggs should not be consumed raw. This book contains some dishes made with
raw or lightly cooked eggs. It is prudent for more vulnerable people, such as pregnant
and nursing mothers, invalids, the elderly, babies and young children, to avoid
uncooked or lightly cooked dishes made with eggs.

This book includes dishes made with nuts and nut derivatives. It is advisable for those
with known allergic reactions to nuts and nut derivatives and those who may be
potentially vulnerable to these allergies, such as pregnant and nursing mothers,
invalids, the elderly, babies and children, to avoid dishes made with nuts and nut oils.
It is also prudent to check the labels of prepared ingredients for the possible inclusion
of nut derivatives.

Contents

Introduction

30 20 10 – quick, quicker, quickest

This book offers a new and flexible approach to meal-planning for busy cooks and lets you choose the recipe option that best fits the time you have available. Inside you will find 360 dishes that will inspire you and motivate you to get cooking every day of the year. All the recipes take a maximum of 30 minutes to cook. Some take as little as 20 minutes and, amazingly, many take only 10 minutes. With a bit of preparation, you can easily try out one new recipe from this book each night and slowly you will build a wide and exciting portfolio of recipes to suit your needs.

How Does It Work?

Every recipe in the QuickCook series can be cooked one of three ways – a 30-minute version, a 20-minute version or a super-quick and easy 10-minute version. At the beginning of each chapter you'll find recipes listed by time. Choose a dish based on how much time you have and turn to that page.

You'll find the main recipe in the middle of the page with a beautiful photograph and two time-variations below.

If you enjoy the dish, you can go back and cook the other time options. If you liked the 30-minute Vanilla, Bran and Blueberry Muffins, but only have 10 minutes to spare, then you'll find a way to cook it using cheat ingredients or clever shortcuts.

If you love the ingredients and flavours of the 10-minute Pan-Fried Salmon with Mixed Bean Salad, why not try something more substantial like the 20-minute Baked Salmon and Mixed Beans, or be inspired to cook a more elaborate version like a Bean and Couscous Salad with Flaked Salmon. Alternatively, browse through all of the 360 delicious recipes, find something that takes your eye – then cook the version that fits your time frame.

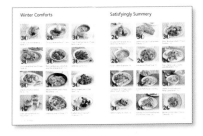

Or, for easy inspiration, turn to the recipe ideas on pages 12–19 to get an instant overview by themes, such as Winter Comforts or Special Occasions.

QuickCook Online

To make life even easier, you can use the special code on each recipe page to email yourself a recipe card for printing, or email a text-only shopping list to your phone. Go to www.hamlynquickcook.com and enter the recipe code at the bottom of each page.

LOW-MEAT-JUU

QuickCook Low Fat

Trying to stick to a diet low in fat can be difficult. People often think that if we leave out all the 'bad stuff' then mealtimes will become boring and not substantial enough to keep us satisfied throughout the day. Leaving us with low energy levels and an increased likelihood to snack; the willpower so necessary in any kind of weight loss programme can quickly fade and the pounds we have worked so hard to lose are quickly regained as we return to our old eating habits.

It has been proven that losing weight slowly and sensibly, through a combination of healthy eating and exercise, is not only much better for our general health, but also that once we have lost the weight, we are much more likely to keep it off. So in order to help you succeed in your own weight loss target and live a healthier life, this book is crammed with low fat, nutritious and substantial recipes which are not only healthy and delicious but also designed to suit any budget, time frame or level of expertise. Whether you are cooking for guests with different dietary needs or just looking for enjoyable family suppers, you will find these recipes flexible enough to suit any occasion and sticking to a diet low in fat will be easier than you imagined.

Tips and Techniques

Changing the way that you cook can dramatically reduce the amount of added fat required. So rather than frying food in lots of oil, try adopting a different cooking method:

- Stir-frying in a hot wok will use a lot less oil and also retains more nutrients than many other ways of cooking.
- Steaming food in a basket or electric steamer uses no oil or added fat at all and is an extremely healthy way to cook.
- Gently poaching is a great, low-fat way of cooking meat and fish whilst keeping it tender and moist.
- Cooking food under a grill or on a ridged griddle pan also uses less fat than frying. It allows excess fat to melt away, gives food a lovely grilled taste and will 'crisp' certain foods such as meat, in a way that some other low-fat cooking methods can't.
- Try using a light oil spray to grease your pans rather than butter or oil. It enables you to fry or roast food without adding too much fat.
- Using a microwave to defrost and reheat food saves time and effort. Try cooking vegetables in a microwave to retain nutrients.
- Cooking food in a pressure cooker will dramatically reduce cooking times and can make your life much easier.
- Try using a flat or ridged panini machine to cook food. As both sides cook at once, this will halve the cooking time.

There a few simple cooking aids that really can have an amazing effect on the time spent in the kitchen.

- A food processor and a mini chopper, are both really useful pieces of equipment which are great time-savers.

- Hand held blenders and jug blenders will purée sauces and soups almost instantly.

- A good vegetable peeler, garlic peeler and crusher are all great, simple little gadgets to help save time on fiddly jobs.

- Using a mandolin slicer to slice vegetables is flexible and fast and will save a lot of time spent preparing food.

- Good, sharp knives make food preparation simpler and faster. If your knives are too blunt, use a knife sharpener to sharpen them.

- Try cooking large amounts and then freezing in portions. This way, you'll always have a fast, ready-made, low-effort meal at your fingertips.

- Preparing ingredients in advance will save time when you come to cook the meal later on. Peel and chop vegetables for example, then keep them refrigerated in freezer bags until you need them.

Ingredients and Storecupboard

To reduce the amount of time spent preparing and cooking, see what healthy alternatives there are available to replace certain ingredients. It is worth bearing in mind that anything pre-prepared this way will usually be more expensive, but as waste is minimal you will often find that it balances out.

- Try using pre-cooked meats and fish such as roast chicken fillets or canned tuna.

- Use frozen prepared vegetables, such as chopped spinach, which are quick and easy and high in nutrients.

- Buy meat which has been been trimmed of excess fat and cut into strips or cubes. This way it is ready to add to a recipe, saving on time and waste.

- Buying a bag of pre-prepared stir-fry vegetables or trimmed, washed and ready-to-cook vegetables will reduce the amount of preparation necessary. The same applies to prepared bags of washed, mixed salads.

- Jars of minced herbs, ginger, garlic, chilli and lemon grass can all be used as substitutes for the 'real thing' and will save on time and washing up!

- You can try using pre-made sauces and dressings but take care to read the ingredients list and nutritional information to make sure there are not too many fats and hidden calories.

- Pre-steamed rice, couscous, pastas and grains and canned pulses and beans are a great base for an almost instant meal.

Winter Comforts

Comforting food for a cold winter's day.

Vanilla, Bran and Blueberry Muffins 28

Crispy Cinnamon French Toast 36

Semi-Dried Tomato and Italian Bean Soup 60

Hot Smoked Trout and Potato Salad 68

Pork and Rosemary Meatballs with Mixed Bean Salad 150

Chilli Con Carne 154

Mild and Creamy Chicken Curry 168

Madeira and Rosemary Pork Medallions 194

Meaty Mushrooms in Red Wine 230

Quick Spiced Rhubarb and Ginger Fool 268

Raspberry Yogurt Gratin 274

Mulled Wine Dried Fruit Compote 278

Satisfyingly Summery

Fresh flavours that capture summer on a plate.

Chunky Fruit Skewers with Rosewater Dressing 30

Butternut Squash and Ricotta Frittata 52

Warm Rainbow Salad with New Potatoes 56

Great Chilled Gazpacho 66

Tomato and Bread Soup 72

Cajun-Spiced Tiger Prawns with Mixed Rice 100

Red Mullet with Capers and a Warm Tomato Salad 104

Sweet Chilli Chicken Stir-Fry 156

Stuffed Pork Steaks with Butter Bean Salad 188

Grilled Vegetable Salad 236

Creamy Stuffed Roast Peppers with Mixed Grains 240

Mediterranean Bowl of Giant Couscous 244

13

Good For Lunch

Healthy dishes for a tasty lunchtime treat.

Wholemeal Bagel with Scrambled Egg and Smoked Salmon 24

Grilled Sourdough with Herby Ricotta and Pancetta 46

Grilled Mushroom and Garlic Wraps 50

Roasted Peppers on Rye 80

Hot and Sour Prawn Soup 90

Soy and Ginger Tuna Fishcakes 98

Smoked Mackerel Pasta Salad 124

Chinese Chicken Wraps with Plum Sauce 148

Serrano Ham and Watercress Salad with Avocado 186

Quinoa-Stuffed Tomatoes with Melting Mozzarella 204

Green Lentil Tapenade with Toast 214

More Than 5 Vegetable Pizza 220

Treat Yourself at the Weekend

Inspiring meals for something a bit different.

Potato and Sweetcorn Hash with Frazzled Eggs 32

American-Style Pancakes with Bacon and Maple Syrup 48

Baked Haddock with Garlic Crumb Crust 126

Tandoori Chicken Skewers with Cucumber Salad 140

Turkey Burger with Spicy Salsa 152

'Meat Feast' Thin and Crispy Pizza 158

Lebanese Lamb Skewers with Cucumber Salad 170

Fast-Seared Steak with French Beans 176

Grilled Barbecue Pork with Coleslaw 198

Lemon Yogurt Cupcakes 258

Blueberry and Orange Eton Mess 260

Individual Chocolate Pots 262

15

Special Occasions

Spectacular dishes for entertaining without the high-fat content.

Mixed Rice and Bean Salad with Smoked Duck Breast 78

Aromatic Steamed Mussels 106

Grilled Scallops with Chermoula Dressing 116

'Roast' Spiced Tuna Loin with Potatoes and Asparagus 128

Griddled Salmon Fillet with Potatoes and Beans 132

Baked Chicken Parcels with Mozzarella and Pesto 160

Roast Pork Tenderloin with Lemon, Sage and Capers 184

Poached Poussin with Baby Vegetables 192

Turkey Breast with Prosciutto 196

Individual Baked Strawberry and Lemon Meringues 250

Baked Figs with Sauternes 266

Baked Nectarines with Vanilla and Cointreau 276

Low Carb

Low-fat and low-carb recipes that don't compromise on taste.

Smoked Ham and Cherry Tomato Omelette 44

Butterflied Sardines with Beetroot Salsa 56

Smoked Chicken with Beans, Walnuts and Tarragon 74

Real Guacamole with Raw Vegetables 76

Pan-Fried Salmon with Mixed Bean Salad 88

Baked Sea Bream with Cumin and Cucumber Yogurt 96

Swordfish Steaks with Basil and Pinenut Oil 102

Lemony Scallop Skewers with Rocket 130

Asian-Spiced Beef Carpaccio 142

Rare Beef and Baby Beetroot Salad 146

Honey and Mustard Chicken Fillets with Coleslaw 164

Marinated Tofu with Sesame Seeds 222

17

Fabulously Fruity

Fresh flavours with a fruity twist.

Apple and Yogurt Muesli 26

Pomegranate and Granola Smoothie 34

Prune and Banana Crunch 40

Lime and Ginger Coleslaw with 5-Spiced Prawns 70

Grilled Sardines with Mango and Lime Salsa 92

Moroccan Grilled Lamb with Sultanas 180

Watermelon, Pomegranate and Halloumi Salad 210

Fragrant Poached Apricots with Pistachios 252

Fresh Berries with Crunchy Oats 254

Sweet and Sour Spiced Pineapple and Mango 256

Cinnamon and Raisin Pear Trifle 264

Quick Kiwi Fruit and Ginger Cheesecake 272

Pasta, Noodles and Rice

Fabulous recipe ideas for storecupboard staples.

Fragrant Soba Noodle Soup 82

Skewered Teriyaki Cod with Steamed Ginger Rice 110

Pasta with Tuna and Aubergine Arrabiata 134

5-Spiced Duck with Ramen Noodles 166

Gnocchi with Smoked Turkey and Blue Cheese 174

Quick Beef Bolognaise 182

Chicken Risotto with White Wine and Asparagus 190

Chilli-Spiked Broccoli with Linguine 206

One-Pot Southern-Style Rice 212

Penne in Tomato, Artichoke and Olive Sauce 216

Vietnamese-Style Vegetable Noodle Salad 228

Lemony Pea Risotto 238

19

QuickCook

Breakfast and Light Bites

Recipes listed by cooking time

10

Wholemeal Bagel with Scrambled Egg and Hot Smoked Salmon

Serves 4

4 hot smoked salmon fillets,
   about 100 g (4½ oz) each
8 eggs
100 ml (3½ fl oz) skimmed milk
1 tablespoon chopped chervil
1 tablespoon chopped chives, plus
   2 tablespoons extra to garnish
25 g (1 oz) low-fat spread
4 wholemeal or multigrain bagels,
   cut in a half
75 g (3 oz) extra light cream
   cheese or ricotta
salt and pepper

- Arrange the smoked salmon fillets on a foil-lined baking sheet, cover with more foil and place in a preheated oven, 180°C (350°F), Gas Mark 4, for 12–15 minutes or until heated through.

- Meanwhile, beat together in a bowl the eggs, milk and herbs and season with salt and pepper.

- Melt the butter in a large, nonstick saucepan over a medium-low heat until frothy, then pour in the egg mixture. Turn the temperature down to very low and, using a heat-resistant rubber spatula, stir the eggs gently for 5–6 minutes or until the eggs are creamy.

- Spilt and toast the bagels, spread the bases thinly with the cream cheese and then spoon over the scrambled eggs.

- Flake the hot smoked salmon fillets over the scrambled egg, and serve, garnished with chives and black pepper.

10 Smoked Salmon with Herbed Scrambled Eggs Beat 8 eggs, 100 ml (3½ fl oz) skimmed milk, 1 tablespoon chopped chervil and 1 tablespoon chopped chives together in a bowl, then cook as above. Meanwhile, toast 4 halved bagels under a medium grill. Spoon the scrambled egg over the toasted bagel and top with 4 slices of thinly sliced smoked salmon. Garnish with snipped chives and serve immediately.

30 Poached Egg with Roasted Smoked Salmon Place 4 lightly smoked salmon fillets in a small, foil-lined roasting tin. Sprinkle over 1 tablespoon chopped chervil, 1 tablespoon chopped chives, pepper and then drizzle with 1 tablespoon extra virgin rapeseed oil. Roast in a preheated oven, 200°C (400°F), Gas Mark 6, for 15–18 minutes until just cooked. Meanwhile, poach 4 eggs, 2 at a time, in a large pan of simmering water for 3 minutes. Arrange 200 g (7 oz) watercress, rocket and spinach salad on 4 serving plates. Flake over the roasted salmon and top each plate with a poached egg. Garnish with snipped chives and pepper and serve with halved toasted bagels.

10 Apple and Yogurt Muesli

Serves 4

400 g (13 oz) fruit and nut muesli (preferably no-added-sugar)

2 dessert apples, such as Granny Smiths, peeled and coarsely grated

450 ml (¾ pint) chilled apple juice

250 g (8 oz) fat-free Greek yogurt with honey

2 teaspoons golden linseeds (optional)

clear honey (optional)

- Place the muesli in a bowl and mix with the apples. Pour over the apple juice, stir well to combine and leave to soak for 5–6 minutes.

- Divide the soaked muesli into serving bowls and spoon the yogurt on top of each one. Scatter over the linseeds, if using, and serve drizzled with some clear honey, if liked.

20 Apple Bircher Muesli

Soak 400 g (13 oz) fruit and nut muesli in 450 ml (¾ pint) hot skimmed milk for 15 minutes while the milk cools. Divide into serving bowls and spoon over 250 g (8 oz) low-fat yogurt. Top each bowl with grated apple from 2 dessert apples and serve sprinkled with 2 teaspoons golden linseeds and a drizzle of clear honey, if liked.

30 Muesli Scones with Apple and Yogurt

Mix 200 g (7 oz) self-raising flour with a pinch of salt in a large bowl. Rub in 50 g (2oz) chilled butter and add 25 g (1 oz) golden caster sugar. Stir in 125 ml (4 fl oz) semi-skimmed milk to form a soft dough, adding 1 tablespoon more milk if necessary. Knead lightly, then place on a lightly floured surface and pat to a thickness of 1.5 cm (¾ inch). Use a 5 cm (2 inch) cookie cutter to cut the dough

into 8–10 rounds, gathering up any remaining dough to make more scones. Place on a lightly greased baking sheet, brush with a little extra milk, sprinkle over 2 tablespoons fruit and nut muesli and bake in a preheated oven, 220°C (425°F), Gas Mark 7, for about 12 minutes or until risen and golden. Remove and transfer to a wire rack to cool slightly, then split the scones in half and serve with grated apple, Greek yogurt with honey and golden linseeds, as liked.

30 Vanilla, Bran and Blueberry Muffins

Makes 12 muffins

250 g (8 oz) plain flour
50 g (2 oz) bran
1 teaspoon baking powder
1 teaspoon bicarbonate soda
3 eggs
1 teaspoon vanilla extract
250 ml (8 fl oz) low-fat
   buttermilk
50 ml (2 fl oz) rice bran oil or
   groundnut oil
125 g (4 oz) blueberries

- Preheat the oven to 180°C (350°F), Gas Mark 4, and lightly grease a 12-cup, nonstick muffin tin or line the muffin tin with paper cake cases.

- In a large bowl mix together the dry ingredients until well combined. Break the eggs into a large jug and beat lightly, then add the vanilla extract, buttermilk and oil.

- Pour the egg mixture into the dry ingredients, add the blueberries and fold gently using a large, metal spoon just until barely combined.

- Use a spring-back ice-cream scoop or large spoon to transfer the batter into the muffin cases.

- Bake in the oven for 18–20 minutes, until risen, golden and firm. Remove from the oven and transfer to a wire rack to cool slightly before serving warm.

 Healthy Blueberry Smoothie

Place 250 g (8 oz) blueberries in a blender with 50 g (2 oz) bran, 125 ml (4 fl oz) low-fat buttermilk, 2 scoops reduced-fat ice cream, 1 teaspoon vanilla extract and 600 ml (1 pint) skimmed milk. Blend until smooth and serve.

 Toasted Blueberry and Seed Muesli

Pour 50 g (2 oz) bran into a large frying pan over a medium heat and dry-fry, stirring frequently, until toasted. Tip into a bowl and then repeat the toasting process with 175 g (6 oz) rolled oats, followed by 50 g (2 oz) sunflower seeds, 50 g (2 oz) pumpkin seeds and 75 g (3 oz) roughly chopped pecan nuts. Add 75 g

(3 oz) dried blueberries and 2 tablespoons dried goji berries or sour cherries to the bowl with the toasted ingredients and stir together until well combined. When completely cool, store the muesli in an airtight container. To serve, stir 1 teaspoon vanilla extract into the desired quantity of skimmed milk and pour over bowls of muesli.

 # Chunky Fruit Skewers with Rosewater Dressing

Serves 4

350 ml (12 fl oz) guava, apple or raspberry and guava juice

2 tablespoons rosewater

3 cardamom pods, lightly crushed

2 star anise

2 tablespoons soft light brown sugar

1 papaya, cut in half, deseeded and cut into chunks

2 kiwifruit, peeled and cut into chunks

1 small pineapple, peeled, cored and cut into chunks

250 g (8 oz) strawberries, hulled and halved if large

- Pour the fruit juice and rosewater into a small saucepan, add the cardamom, star anise and sugar and place over a low heat. Stir to dissolve the sugar, then simmer gently for 5–6 minutes until fragrant. Pour into a large, shallow bowl and set aside to cool.

- Meanwhile, thread the chunks of papaya, kiwifruit and pineapple alternately on to 8 skewers and arrange 2 skewers per person on serving plates.

- Strain the dressing into a jug to remove the spices and drizzle over the fruit skewers before serving.

 Tropical Fruit and Rosewater Juice
Prepare ½ small pineapple, 2 kiwifruit, 1 papaya and 250 g (8 oz) strawberries, as above, and put in a blender with a pinch of ground cardamom and 750 ml (17 fl oz) guava juice. Blend until smooth, then stir in 2 tablespoons rosewater. Fill tall glasses with ice cubes, add 1 whole star anise to each glass and then pour in the fruit juice. Serve immediately.

 Mixed Fruit Crumble with a Spicy Guava Syrup Mix together in a large bowl 75 g (3 oz) plain flour and ½ teaspoon ground ginger. Stir in 50 g (2 oz) melted butter, 75 g (3 oz) rolled oats, 50 g (2 oz) demerara sugar and 2 tablespoons desiccated coconut. In a separate bowl, toss together 1 pineapple, 2 kiwifruit, 1 papaya and 250 g (8 oz) strawberries, prepared as above. Tip the fruits into an ovenproof dish, scatter the oat topping evenly over the top and gently press down. Bake in a preheated oven, 200°C (400°F), Gas Mark 6, for about 20 minutes or until the fruit is tender and the topping crispy. Meanwhile, make the spiced syrup as above, using 350 ml (12 fl oz) guava juice, 2 tablespoons rosewater, 3 lightly crushed cardamom pods, 2 star anise and 2 tablespoons soft light brown sugar. Serve the crumble drizzled with the warm syrup and a dollop of fat-free Greek yogurt. Sprinkle over desiccated coconut and drizzle with clear honey, if liked.

30 Potato and Sweetcorn Hash with Frazzled Eggs

Serves 4

750 g (1½ lb) large potatoes, peeled and diced
2 tablespoons light olive oil
1 large onion, finely chopped
1 large green pepper, deseeded and chopped
1 teaspoon smoked paprika
200 g (7 oz) can sweetcorn, drained
olive oil spray
4 large eggs
2 tablespoons snipped chives
salt and pepper

- Put the potatoes in a large saucepan and cover with lightly salted water. Bring to the boil and cook for 12–15 minutes until tender, then drain in a colander.

- Meanwhile, heat the oil in a large, nonstick frying pan with an ovenproof handle over a medium heat. Add the onion and green pepper and cook, stirring occasionally, for 7–8 minutes until softened and lightly golden. Add the cooked potatoes, smoked paprika and sweetcorn, season generously with salt and pepper and cook for 3–4 minutes, stirring frequently.

- Slide the pan under a preheated grill, keeping the handle away from the heat, and grill for 2–3 minutes until crispy.

- While the hash is grilling, spray a large frying pan with the oil then place over a medium heat. Crack the eggs into the pan and fry for 3 minutes until the egg whites are set and crispy.

- Using a fish slice, lift the eggs on to the hash in the pan and return under the grill to cook the yolk, if desired. Serve immediately sprinkled with the chives.

10 Warm Salad with Frazzled Eggs

Pan-fry 1 finely chopped onion and 1 chopped green pepper in 1 tablespoon oil, as above. One minute before the end of cooking, add 200 g (7 oz) can sweetcorn, drained, and 1 teaspoon smoked paprika. Meanwhile 'frazzle' the eggs as above. Toss the vegetables with 150 g (5 oz) crunchy salad leaves and 1 tablespoon red wine vinegar and arrange on serving plates. Top the salad with a frazzled egg and serve sprinkled with snipped chives.

20 Spanish-Style Sweetcorn Tortilla

Thinly slice 500 g (1 lb) small potatoes and cook in lightly salted boiling water for 10–12 minutes until tender. Meanwhile, pan-fry 1 finely chopped large onion and 1 large deseeded and chopped green pepper in 1 tablespoon light olive oil, as above. Add 1 teaspoon smoked paprika and 200 g (7 oz) can sweetcorn, drained, and cook for a further minute. Beat 6 eggs in a bowl and season generously with salt and pepper. Drain the potatoes and stir into the pan with the onions and peppers. Add the eggs, cover loosely and cook for 3–4 minutes, without stirring. Invert the tortilla on to a plate and slide back into the pan for a further 3–4 minutes until firm. Slide on to a board and serve in wedges.

10 Pomegranate and Granola Smoothie

Serves 4

750 ml (1¼ pint) pomegranate juice

2 tablespoons pomegranate molasses

500 g (1 lb) fresh or frozen mango pieces

125 g (4 oz) granola

1–2 tablespoons agave nectar or runny honey

4 scoops fat-free frozen yogurt

100 g (3½ oz) pomegranate seeds (optional)

- Place all the ingredients except the frozen yogurt and pomegranate seeds, if using, in a blender and blend until smooth. This may need to be done in 2 batches.

- Take 4 glasses and place 1 scoop of frozen yogurt in each. Pour the smoothie over the yogurt, sprinkle over pomegranate seeds, if using, and serve immediately.

20 Fruit Salad with Pomegranate Syrup

Place 350 ml (12 fl oz) pomegranate juice in a saucepan with 1–2 tablespoons agave nectar or clear honey, to taste, and the seeds scraped from 1 vanilla pod. Simmer for 4–5 minutes until thickened, then remove from the heat. Meanwhile, peel and cut up the flesh of ¼ watermelon into large chunks, removing any seeds. Mix with 200 g (7 oz) halved seedless grapes, 350 g (11½ oz) fresh or frozen mango pieces and 2 peeled and thickly sliced kiwi fruit in a large bowl. Spoon into serving dishes and top with a scoop of fat-free frozen yogurt, if liked. Scatter with 100 g (3½ oz) pomegranate seeds, if liked, and drizzle with 2 tablespoons pomegranate syrup. Serve immediately.

30 Quinoa Porridge with Pomegranate

Place 250 g (8 oz) uncooked quinoa in a saucepan with 1 litre (1¾ pints) skimmed milk, 1–2 tablespoons agave nectar or clear honey, to taste, and 2 tablespoons pomegranate molasses. Bring to the boil, cover, reduce the heat to low and simmer gently, stirring occasionally, for 15–20 minutes until tender and creamy. Stir in 1 teaspoon rosewater and then spoon into serving bowls. Serve with a spoonful of fat-free Greek yogurt and scattered with 100 g (3½ oz) pomegranate seeds.

 # Crispy Cinnamon French Toast

Serves 4

3 eggs
50 ml (2 fl oz) skimmed milk
½ teaspoon ground cinnamon
25 g (1 oz) butter
8 slices raisin and cinnamon loaf
  or 4 low-fat hot cross buns
8 tablespoons demerara or
  cinnamon sugar
4 scoops of reduced-fat
  ice-cream or frozen yogurt,
  to serve (optional)

- In a large, shallow bowl, beat the eggs with the milk and cinnamon. Melt half the butter in a large, nonstick frying pan over a medium heat.

- Dip 4 slices of the bread in the egg mixture and sprinkle both sides with half the sugar. Alternatively, cut the hot cross buns in half horizontally and dip 4 halves in the egg and then sprinkle with the sugar.

- Place the coated bread in the pan of melted butter and cook gently for 4–6 minutes, turning once, until golden and crispy. Drain on kitchen paper and keep warm. Repeat the process with the remaining slices of bread.

- Serve 2 slices of French toast per person with a scoop of ice-cream or frozen yogurt.

 Crunchy Granola with Cinnamon and Apple Divide 300 g (10 oz) crunchy granola among 4 bowls. Peel, core and dice 2 dessert apples, such as Granny Smiths, and scatter the apple over the muesli with 75 g (3 oz) golden raisins. Stir 1 teaspoon ground cinnamon into 250 g (8 oz) fat-free Greek yogurt with honey, then spoon into the bowls. Serve sprinkled with cinnamon sugar, if liked.

 Cinnamon and Raisin Pastries Beat 1 egg with 1 tablespoon skimmed milk and brush over a 375 g (12 oz) rectangle of ready-rolled, reduced-fat puff pastry. Scatter over 1 teaspoon ground cinnamon, 75 g (3 oz) golden raisins and 4 tablespoons cinnamon sugar. Roll up the pastry and cut into 1 cm (½ inch) rounds. Place the rounds on a large, lightly greased baking sheet, leaving space for them to expand, flatten slightly and brush again with the remaining the egg wash. Sprinkle with 1 tablespoon cinnamon sugar and cook in a preheated oven, 200°C (400°C), Gas Mark 6, for about 20 minutes or until crisp and golden.

30 Moroccan Baked Eggs

Serves 4

1 tablespoon olive oil
1 onion, chopped
2 garlic cloves, sliced
1 teaspoon ras el hanout
¼ teaspoon ground cinnamon
1 teaspoon ground coriander
800 g (1 lb 12 oz) can cherry
  tomatoes
4 tablespoons chopped coriander
4 eggs
salt and pepper

- Preheat the oven to 220°C (425°F), Gas Mark 7. Heat the olive oil in a frying pan over a medium heat, add the onion and garlic and cook for 6–7 minutes or until softened and lightly golden, stirring occasionally.

- Stir in the spices and cook for a further minute, then add the cherry tomatoes. Season generously with salt and pepper, then simmer gently for 8–10 minutes. Scatter over 3 tablespoons of the coriander.

- Divide the tomato mixture into 4 individual ovenproof dishes, then crack an egg into each dish. Cook in the oven for 8–10 minutes until the egg is set but the yolks are still slightly runny. Cook for a further 2–3 minutes if you prefer the eggs to be cooked through.

- Serve scattered with the remaining coriander and plenty of crusty bread on the side.

10 Moroccan Fried Eggs with Spinach

Heat 1 tablespoon olive oil in a large frying pan over a medium heat. Add 1 teaspoon ras el hanout, ¼ teaspoon ground cinnamon and 1 teaspoon ground coriander and fry for 1 minute. Crack 4 eggs into the pan and cook for 3–5 minutes or until cooked to your liking. Meanwhile, toast 4 slices of crusty bread and place a handful of baby leaf spinach on each. Scatter over 4 halved cherry tomatoes per person and sprinkle over chopped coriander. Lift the fried eggs on to the spinach and serve.

20 Pan-Baked Moroccan Eggs

Heat 1 tablespoon olive oil in a frying pan over a medium heat. Add 1 chopped onion and 2 sliced garlic cloves and cook for 6–7 minutes until softened. Add 1 teaspoon ras el hanout, ¼ teaspoon ground cinnamon and 1 teaspoon ground coriander and cook for 1 minute, then add 800 g (1 lb 12 oz) can cherry tomatoes and season with salt and pepper. Gently simmer for about 6–7 minutes or until fragrant, then add 3 tablespoons chopped coriander. Make 4 shallow wells in the surface of

the tomato sauce and crack an egg into each. Cover the pan with a lid and cook for 3–4 minutes or until the eggs are cooked to your liking. Transfer to serving plates with 1 egg per person, scatter over 1 tablespoon chopped coriander and serve.

1 Prune and Banana Crunch

Serves 4

2 firm, ripe bananas, diced

350 g (11½ oz) ready-to-eat stoned prunes

2 teaspoons clear honey (optional)

500 g (1 lb) fat-free Greek yogurt

75 g (3 oz) cornflakes or crunchy cereal flakes

- Combine the bananas, prunes, honey and yogurt in a large bowl.

- Spoon into attractive glass bowls and top with the cornflakes or crunch cereal flakes. Serve immediately with glasses of apple juice, if liked.

 2 Banana Yogurt and Prune Compote with Muesli Roughly chop 350 g (11½ oz) ready-to-eat stoned prunes and place in a small pan with 200 ml (7 fl oz) prune juice, 2 teaspoons clear honey, finely grated rind of ½ orange, 2 cloves and ½ cinnamon stick. Place over a low heat and simmer for 5–6 minutes until thick and sticky. Set aside to cool for 8–10 minutes. While cooling, mash 2 firm, ripe bananas into 500 g (1 lb) fat-free Greek yogurt. Spoon the banana yogurt into serving bowls over the desired amounts of healthy granola or muesli. Remove the spices from the prune compote and spoon over the yogurt. Serve immediately.

 3 Banana and Prune Muffins Put 250 g (8 oz) self-raising flour, 1 teaspoon baking powder, 125 g (4 oz) soft dark brown sugar, 2 lightly beaten eggs, 200 ml (7 fl oz) skimmed milk, 75 ml (3 fl oz) vegetable oil, 1 mashed banana and 100 g (3½ oz) chopped, ready-to-eat stoned prunes into a large bowl. Beat to combine, then spoon into the cups of a lightly greased nonstick 12-cup muffin tin. Cook in a preheated oven, 200°C (400°F), Gas Mark 6, for 18–20 minutes until golden, risen and firm to the touch. Remove from the oven and transfer to a wire rack to cool slightly before serving.

30 American-Style Giant Apple and Cinnamon Muffins

Makes 6

butter, for greasing
200 g (7 oz) wholemeal flour
50 g (2 oz) fine oatmeal
1 teaspoon baking powder
1 teaspoon bicarbonate of soda
½ teaspoon ground cinnamon
100 g (3½ oz) soft light
   brown sugar
pinch of salt
200 g (7 oz) apple, apple
   and apricot, or apple and
   blueberry purée
150 ml (¼ pint) buttermilk
3 tablespoons groundnut oil
2 large eggs, lightly beaten

- Preheat the oven to 180°C (350°F), Gas Mark 4, and lightly grease a 6-cup nonstick giant muffin tin.

- In a large bowl, mix together all the dry ingredients.

- Beat the remaining ingredients together in a large jug and pour into the dry mixture. Use a large metal spoon to stir until barely combined, then spoon the batter into the prepared muffin tin. Place in the oven for 20–22 minutes until risen, firm and golden. Remove from the oven and transfer the muffins to a wire rack to cool slightly before serving warm.

 Apple and Cinnamon Oaty Yogurt

Mix together 200 g (7 oz) apple purée and ½ teaspoon cinnamon in a bowl, then fold into 300 g (10 oz) fat-free Greek yogurt with honey. Serve sprinkled with 50 g (2 oz) rolled oats and a little soft light brown sugar, if liked.

 Cinnamon Stewed Apples

Peel, core and dice 3 Bramley apples, about 500 g (1 lb) total weight. Place in a saucepan with ½ teaspoon cinnamon, 2 tablespoons soft light brown sugar and 1 tablespoon apple juice. Warm over a medium heat for 5–6 minutes until the apples collapse. Cool slightly, then serve with the desired quantity of healthy muesli.

Smoked Ham and Cherry Tomato Omelette

Serves 4

4 teaspoons extra virgin rapeseed oil

4 shallots, thinly sliced

8 eggs, lightly beaten

2 tablespoons chopped mixed herbs, such as chives, chervil, parsley, basil and thyme

200 g (7 oz) yellow and red cherry tomatoes, cut in half

150 g (5 oz) wafer-thin slices smoked ham

salt and pepper

- Heat 1 teaspoon of the oil in a medium-sized frying pan over a medium-low heat. Add the shallots and cook gently for 4–5 minutes or until softened.

- Meanwhile, beat together the eggs and herbs in a large jug and season with salt and pepper.

- Remove three-quarters of the shallots from the pan with a slotted spoon and pour over one-quarter of the egg mixture. Scatter over one-quarter of the cherry tomatoes and stir gently, using a heat-resistant rubber spatula, until the egg is almost set.

- Scatter one-quarter of the sliced ham evenly over the top of the omelette and cook gently for a further minute. Fold the omelette in half and slide out of the pan on to a warmed plate. Serve immediately and repeat the process to make 3 more omelettes. Alternatively, keep the cooked omelettes warm until all 4 are ready and serve at the same time.

Smoked Ham and Tomato Frittata

In a large frying pan with an ovenproof handle melt 15 g (½ oz) butter over a medium heat until frothy. Add 8 lightly beaten eggs to the pan, 2 tablespoons chopped mixed herbs, selection as above, and 200 g (7 oz) halved yellow and red cherry tomatoes and gently stir together. Add 150 g (5 oz) roughly chopped wafer-thin slices smoked ham and continue stirring gently for 2–3 minutes until almost set. Sprinkle over 2 tablespoons grated Parmesan cheese, then place under a preheated medium grill for 3–4 minutes until set and golden. Serve in wedges with salad leaves.

Smoked Ham and Tomato Flan

Beat 6 eggs with 2 tablespoons chopped mixed herbs, selection as above, and season with salt and pepper. Spread 150 g (5 oz) wafer-thin slices smoked ham over the base of a 23 cm (9 inch) pre-baked pastry case, then pour in the egg mixture. Scatter over 200 g (7 oz) halved cherry tomatoes, then sprinkle over 2 tablespoons grated Parmesan cheese. Place in a preheated oven, 200°C (400°F), Gas Mark 6, for 20–25 minutes until set and golden.

Grilled Sourdough with Herby Ricotta and Crispy Pancetta

Serves 4

4 large slices sourdough bread
8 slices lean pancetta
75 g (3 oz) ready-to-eat,
  slow-roasted tomatoes
  (not in oil), chopped
2 tablespoons toasted pine nuts
  (optional)
rocket leaves, to garnish

Herby Ricotta Filling

250 g (8 oz) ricotta or extra light
  cream cheese
2 spring onions, finely chopped
4 tablespoons chopped mixed
  herbs, such as chervil, chives,
  parsley, basil, marjoram and
  tarragon
finely grated rind of 1 lemon
1 tablespoon lemon juice
salt and pepper

- For the herby ricotta filling, mix together the ricotta or cream cheese with the spring onions, mixed herbs and lemon rind and juice. Season with salt and pepper and set aside.

- Heat a ridged griddle pan and toast the slices of bread in 2 batches for 3–4 minutes each batch, turning once, or until toasted and lightly charred. Keep warm.

- Leave the pan on the heat and add the pancetta. Griddle for 2–3 minutes, turning once, until crispy. Drain any excess fat on kitchen paper.

- Spread the toast thickly with the ricotta mixture and arrange on serving plates. Scatter over the slow-roasted tomatoes and the pine nuts, if using, then top with the slices of crispy pancetta. Garnish with a few rocket leaves and serve.

 Warmed Ricotta and Slow-Roasted Tomato Open Sandwiches
Make up the herby ricotta filling, as above. Spread the ricotta over 4 large slices sourdough bread, then place on a grill rack under a preheated medium grill for 3–4 minutes until heated through. Remove and layer over 8 slices of lean Parma ham. Scatter with 75 g (3 oz) rocket leaves and 75 g (3 oz) chopped ready-to-eat, slow-roasted tomatoes (not in oil). Serve.

 Herby Ricotta Tomato Toasts
Make up the herby ricotta filling as above, then mix in 200 g (7 oz) chopped, drained, roasted red peppers and 2 tablespoons toasted pine nuts. Cut the tops off 4 large beef tomatoes and scoop out the seeds. Stuff the tomatoes with the ricotta filling and transfer the tomatoes to a baking sheet. Bake in a preheated oven, 190°C (375°F) Gas Mark 5, for 20–22 minutes or until the tomatoes are tender. Meanwhile, griddle 4 large slices sourdough bread as above, then cut 1 garlic clove in half and rub the cut edges over the toasted bread. Grill 8 slices lean pancetta on the hot griddle pan until crispy. Serve the stuffed tomatoes on the garlicky toast, topped with crispy pancetta and each one drizzled with 1 teaspoon balsamic syrup.

30 American-Style Pancakes with Bacon and Maple Syrup

Serves 4

200 g (7 oz) self-raising flour
1 teaspoon baking powder
pinch of cinnamon
1 egg, lightly beaten
150 ml (¼ pint) buttermilk
100 ml (3½ fl oz) skimmed milk
1 teaspoon vanilla extract
8 slices lean, smoked streaky
   bacon
15 g (½ oz) butter
2–4 tablespoons maple syrup,
   to serve

- Sift the flour, baking powder and cinnamon into a bowl and make a well in the centre. Pour in the eggs, buttermilk, skimmed milk and vanilla extract and beat to a smooth batter.

- Place the bacon on a foil-lined baking sheet under a preheated grill for 5–6 minutes or until the fat has melted away and the bacon is crispy. Keep warm.

- Melt a little butter in a large, nonstick frying pan over a medium heat and pour 4 spoonfuls of batter into the pan to make 4 small, thick pancakes. Cook for 2–3 minutes, then flip over and cook for a further 2–3 minutes until golden. Remove and repeat the process to make 12 pancakes, or until the batter is finished, stacking up the pancakes and keeping them warm.

- Serve the pancakes in little piles with the crispy bacon and drizzled with the maple syrup.

 Scotch Pancakes with Bacon and Maple Syrup Heat 8 ready-made Scotch pancakes according to the packet instructions. Grill 8 slices bacon as in the 30-minute variation and serve with the warmed pancakes, drizzled with the maple syrup.

 Banana Pancakes and Maple Syrup Sift 200 g (7 oz) self-raising flour, 1 teaspoon baking powder and a pinch of cinnamon into a bowl and mix with 1 tablespoon caster sugar, 1 lightly beaten egg, 150 ml (¼ pint) buttermilk, 100 ml (3½ fl oz) skimmed milk and 1 teaspoon vanilla extract to make a batter as above. Mash 1 banana with a fork and stir into the batter with 125 g (4 oz) raspberries. Cook the pancakes until golden as above. Serve in stacks with reduced-fat ice cream and drizzled with warmed maple syrup.

# Grilled Mushroom and Garlic Wraps

Serves 4

500 g (1 lb) large, flat field mushrooms, thickly sliced

2 garlic cloves, finely chopped

3 spring onions, trimmed and thinly sliced

2 tablespoons olive oil

100 g (3½ oz) extra light cream cheese

4 large, low-fat or multiseed soft tortilla wrap breads

4 tablespoons chopped chives

12 cherry tomatoes, cut into quarters

2 romaine lettuce hearts, shredded, plus extra to serve (optional)

salt and pepper

- Toss the mushrooms with the garlic, spring onions and olive oil in a large bowl. Season with salt and pepper, then tip on to a nonstick baking sheet and place under a preheated medium grill for 6–8 minutes until golden and tender, turning frequently.

- Meanwhile, spread the cream cheese over the tortilla wraps and scatter over the chives.

- Place the sliced mushrooms on the centre of each wrap, then scatter over the cherry tomatoes and top with a handful of the lettuce. Fold the edges of the wrap into the centre to completely enclose the filling, creating 4 parcels.

- Heat a large, ridged griddle pan over a medium-high heat. Place the parcels on the griddle and toast for 4–5 minutes, turning occasionally, until nicely charred on both sides. This may need to be done in two batches.

- Cut in half diagonally and serve immediately.

 Quick Mushroom, Cream Cheese and Chive Wraps Heat 1 tablespoon olive oil in a frying pan over a medium heat, and cook 500 g (1 lb) thickly sliced, large, flat field mushrooms with 2 finely chopped garlic cloves for 5–6 minutes. Meanwhile, spread 4 low-fat soft tortilla wraps with 100 g (3½ oz) extra light cream cheese and scatter with snipped chives. Top the tortillas with the cooked mushrooms, 12 quartered cherry tomatoes, shredded lettuce and 3 thinly sliced spring onions. Roll up tightly, cut in half and serve.

 Baked Mushroom Wraps in Hot Salsa Sauce Heat 1 tablespoon olive oil in a frying pan over a medium heat, then cook 500 g (1 lb) large, flat field mushrooms, thickly sliced, with 2 finely chopped garlic cloves for 5–6 minutes until tender. Spread 4 low-fat or multiseed soft tortilla wrap breads with 100 g (3½ oz) extra light cream cheese and spoon over the cooked mushrooms and 12 quartered cherry tomatoes. Roll up and place in an ovenproof dish in a single layer. Pour over a 300 g (10 oz) jar chunky tomato salsa and scatter with 3 thinly sliced spring onions and 2 tablespoons sliced jalapeños in brine. Bake in a preheated oven, 200°C (400°F), Gas Mark 6, for 15–18 minutes until hot. Meanwhile, mix together 6 tablespoons low-fat soured cream, 2 tablespoons lime juice and 2 tablespoons snipped chives in a small bowl. Season with salt and pepper. Dress 2 shredded romaine lettuce hearts in the dressing and arrange on serving plates with the wraps.

30 Butternut Squash and Ricotta Frittata

Serves 4

1 tablespoon extra virgin rapeseed oil

1 red onion, thinly sliced

450 g (14½ oz) peeled butternut squash, diced

8 eggs

1 tablespoon chopped thyme

2 tablespoons chopped sage

125 g (4 oz) ricotta

salt and pepper

- Heat the oil in a large, deep frying pan with an ovenproof handle over a medium-low heat, then add the onion and butternut squash. Cover loosely and cook gently, stirring frequently, for 18–20 minutes or until softened and golden.

- Beat the eggs lightly with the thyme, sage and ricotta, then season generously with salt and pepper and pour over the butternut squash.

- Cook for a further 2–3 minutes until the egg is almost set, stirring occasionally with a heat-resistant rubber spatula to prevent the base from burning.

- Slide the pan under a preheated grill, keeping the handle away from the heat, and grill for 3–4 minutes, or until the egg is set and the frittata is golden. Slice into wedges and serve with a baby leaf salad.

 Strawberry and Ricotta Pancakes

Beat 4 tablespoons strawberry jam with 250 g (8 oz) ricotta. Warm 8 ready-made thin pancakes, according to the packet instructions, spread the ricotta mixture over the pancakes, then roll up loosely and place in an ovenproof dish. Dust with 1 tablespoon vanilla sugar and slide under a preheated hot grill for 2–3 minutes until warm. Serve immediately with 200 g (7 oz) sliced strawberries.

 Courgette and Pea Frittata Heat 1 tablespoon extra virgin rapeseed oil in a frying pan over a medium heat, then add 1 thinly sliced red onion and stir-fry for 1 minute. Add 2 diced courgettes and cook for a further 4–5 minutes until softened, then stir in 150 g (5 oz) frozen petit pois and cook for 1–2 minutes until thawed. Meanwhile, beat the eggs lightly with 2 tablespoons chopped mint, then add 200 g (7 oz) cubed reduced-fat feta and season

generously with salt and pepper. Pour the egg mixture over the courgettes and peas and cook for 2–3 minutes, stirring occasionally. Slide under a preheated hot grill for 2–3 minutes or until the eggs are set and golden. Serve in wedges with a baby leaf salad.

LOW-LIGH-WEF

10 Broad Bean and Mint Hummus with Wholegrain Crostini

Serves 4

250 g (8 oz) frozen peas

250 g (8 oz) frozen baby broad beans, preferably peeled

1 wholegrain or granary baguette, sliced

125 g (4 oz) fat-free Greek yogurt

2 tablespoons lemon juice

2 tablespoons chopped mint

salt and pepper

toasted sesame seeds, to garnish

- Put the peas and beans in a bowl and pour over enough boiling water to cover completely. Cover with a plate and set aside for 3 minutes. Drain and quickly cool under running cold water.

- Meanwhile, place the slices of wholegrain baguette under a preheated grill to toast for 1–2 minutes each side until golden brown.

- Place the peas and beans in a food processor or blender. Add the yogurt, lemon juice and 1 tablespoon of the mint and blend until almost smooth. Scrape into a bowl and stir through the remaining mint, then season with salt and pepper.

- Spoon the pea and mint hummus into small bowls, scatter over toasted sesame seeds and serve with the toasted baguette slices.

20 Warm Pea and Broad Bean Salad

with New Potatoes Cook 500 g (1 lb) new potatoes in boiling water for 15–18 minutes until tender. Meanwhile, bring a saucepan of water to the boil and cook 250 g (8 oz) each peas and beans for 3–4 minutes until tender. Drain and place in a large bowl with 2 finely sliced spring onions, 2 tablespoons chopped mint, 2 tablespoons lemon juice, 2 tablespoons olive oil, 75 g (3 oz) chopped, ready-to-eat slow roasted tomatoes (not in oil) and salt and pepper. Tip in the potatoes, toss gently, and serve warm.

30 Baby Broad Bean and Pea Tart

Cook 150 g (5 oz) each of frozen baby broad beans and frozen peas in boiling water for 3–4 minutes until tender. Cool under running cold water, drain well and set aside. Place a 375 g (12 oz) sheet of ready-rolled puff pastry on a baking sheet and use a sharp knife to score a 2.5 cm (1 inch) border around the edge. Spread 150 g (5 oz) low-fat cream cheese with chives over the pastry, keeping within the border. Scatter over the beans and peas and 2 finely sliced spring onions. Season

generously with salt and pepper and crumble 150 g (5 oz) reduced-fat feta cheese over the top. Cook in a preheated oven, 200°C (400°F), Gas Mark 6, for 20 minutes, or until golden. Serve in slices with mixed salad leaves.

30 Warm Rainbow Salad with New Potatoes and Walnut Dressing

Serves 4

300 g (10 oz) baby new potatoes
1 red pepper, deseeded and sliced
1 yellow pepper, deseeded and sliced
1 tablespoon olive oil
3 sprigs fresh thyme
1 large raw beetroot, peeled and coarsely grated
1 large carrot, coarsely grated
150 g (5 oz) colourful mixed salad leaves
2 tablespoons crushed walnuts (optional)
salt and pepper

Dressing

2 tablespoons walnut oil
1 tablespoon shallot vinegar
1 tablespoon Dijon mustard
pinch of sugar

- Preheat the oven to 190 °C (375 °F), Gas Mark 5. Toss the potatoes and peppers in the olive oil with the thyme sprigs and season with plenty of salt and pepper. Tip into a large roasting tin and place in the oven for 20–25 minutes until tender. Meanwhile, combine the beetroot and carrot with the salad leaves and divide among 4 serving plates.

- To make the dressing, put all the ingredients and a pinch of salt and pepper into a jar with a tight-fitting lid. Shake well to combine.

- Remove the roasting tin from the oven and discard the thyme. Arrange the vegetables on to the plates on top of the salad leaves and drizzle with the dressing. Scatter over the walnuts, if using, and serve immediately.

 Quick Rainbow Salad with Walnut Dressing Make the dressing, as above. Arrange 150 g (5 oz) colourful mixed salad leaves on 4 serving plates and scatter over 1 thinly sliced red pepper and 1 thinly sliced yellow pepper. Coarsely grate 1 peeled beetroot, 1 carrot and 1 yellow or green courgette. Arrange over the salad leaves and peppers and drizzle with the dressing. Scatter with 2 tablespoons crushed walnuts, if liked, and serve.

 Rainbow Stir-Fry with Noodles Cut 1 large peeled beetroot and 2 carrots into matchsticks, deseed and thinly slice 1 red and 1 yellow pepper and thickly slice 1 red onion. Cook 375 g (12 oz) medium egg noodles according to the packet instructions until 'al dente' and drain into a colander. Heat 2 teaspoons sesame oil in a large wok or frying pan over a medium heat and stir-fry the onion for 30 seconds before adding the beetroot, carrots

and peppers. Stir-fry for 3–4 minutes until beginning to soften. Tip in the drained noodles and toss with the vegetables, adding 250 ml (8 fl oz) sweet chilli stir-fry sauce, if liked. Heap on to serving plates and scatter over 1 tablespoon golden sesame seeds to serve.

Butterflied Sardines with Beetroot Salsa

Serves 4

4 tablespoons finely chopped parsley
finely grated rind of 1 lemon
2 teaspoons lemon juice
1 teaspoon harissa
2 garlic cloves, finely chopped
1 tablespoon extra virgin rapeseed oil
8–12 scaled and butterflied sardines (you can ask your fishmonger to do this for you)
2 tablespoons snipped dill
salt and cracked black pepper

Beetroot salsa

350 g (11½ oz) cooked beetroot (not in vinegar), diced
½ red onion, very finely chopped
1 tablespoon aged sherry vinegar
2 tablespoons baby capers, rinsed and drained

- Mix together 2 tablespoons of the parsley, the lemon rind and juice, the harissa, garlic and oil. Season with cracked black pepper, then rub the marinade over the sardines and set aside.

- To make the beetroot salsa mix together all the ingredients and season with salt and pepper.

- Lay the sardines on a grill tray and slide under a preheated grill for 2–3 minutes, turning once, or until cooked through.

- Arrange the sardines on serving plates with the beetroot salsa and scattered with the dill. Serve with toasted slices of ciabatta on the side.

 Sardine, Chickpea and Beetroot Salad
Prepare the beetroot salsa as above, adding 400 g (13 oz) can chickpeas, drained. Toss through 250 g (8 oz) baby leaf and herb salad. Drain 2 x 120 g (4 oz) cans sardines and scatter the sardines over the salad. Divide the salad between 4 serving plates and sprinkle with 2 tablespoons snipped dill.

 Linguine with Sardines and Beetroot Cook 400 g (13 oz) linguine for 11 minutes until 'al dente', or according to the packet instructions. Meanwhile, mix together 2 tablespoons finely chopped parsley, finely grated rind of 1 lemon, 1 teaspoon harissa, 2 finely chopped garlic cloves and 1 tablespoon extra virgin rapeseed oil. Place 16 fresh sardine fillets on a nonstick baking sheet. Rub the marinade over the sardine fillets, then slide them under a preheated grill for 2–3 minutes until cooked and slightly charred, turning once. Flake the sardines roughly into a bowl, add 200 g (7 oz) finely diced cooked beetroot (not in vinegar), 2 tablespoons chopped parsley, 2 teaspoons lemon juice, 2 tablespoons baby capers and 1 finely chopped red chilli and mix together. Drain the linguine and toss through the sardine mixture until well combined, then serve.

30 Semi-Dried Tomato and Italian Bean Soup

Serves 4

1 tablespoon olive oil
1 large onion, chopped
4 garlic cloves, roughly chopped
2 sticks celery, trimmed and
   roughly chopped
1 carrot, diced
400 g (13 oz) can peeled cherry
   tomatoes
8 ready-to-eat slow-roasted
   tomatoes (not in oil), chopped
350 g (11½ oz) Tuscan bean mix
   or 400 g (13 oz) can mixed
   beans, drained
1 tablespoon chopped oregano
750 ml (1¼ pints) vegetable stock
4 tablespoons ricotta
reduced-fat pesto or basil oil,
   to drizzle (optional)
salt and pepper

- Heat the oil in a large, heavy-based pan over a medium heat, then add the onion, garlic, celery and carrots. Loosely cover and cook over a medium heat for 7–8 minutes, stirring occasionally, until softened and lightly coloured.

- Add the cherry and slow-roasted tomatoes, beans, oregano and stock and bring to the boil. Reduce the heat slightly and simmer gently for 18 minutes, or until the vegetables are tender and the flavours have developed. Blend with a hand blender until smooth, then season with salt and pepper.

- Ladle the soup into bowls and serve topped with a spoonful of ricotta and a drizzle of pesto or basil oil, if liked, and crusty French bread.

1 Italian Bean Salad

Mix together 350 g (11½ oz) Tuscan bean mix with 2 thinly sliced spring onions, 8 chopped ready-to-eat slow-roasted tomatoes (not in oil), 2 thinly sliced celery sticks and 1 coarsely grated carrot. Toss with 1 tablespoon reduced-fat pesto, 2 tablespoons lemon juice and 125 g (4 oz) rocket leaves. Season generously with salt and pepper, then sprinkle over 2 tablespoons each of roughly chopped oregano and basil. Serve with crusty baguette.

2 Quick Rustic Bean Soup

Heat 1 tablespoon olive oil in a large, heavy-based pan over a medium heat, then add 1 chopped large onion and 4 roughly chopped garlic cloves and cook for 4–5 minutes or until softened. Add 400 g (13 oz) can mixed beans, drained, 2 tablespoons sun-dried tomato paste, 400 g (13 oz) can peeled cherry tomatoes, 750 ml (1¼ pints) vegetable stock and 1 tablespoon chopped oregano. Bring to the boil, then reduce the heat and simmer for 12–14 minutes until hot and fragrant. Ladle the soup into serving bowls and top each bowl with a spoonful of ricotta and a drizzle of reduced-fat pesto.

10 Quick Mushroom and Brown Rice Bowl

Serves 4

1 tablespoon olive oil
8 portabellini or small flat field
  mushrooms, chopped
1 teaspoon chopped tarragon
350 g (12 ½ oz) cooked roast
  chicken slices, roughly chopped
500 g (1 lb) steamed brown
  basmati rice
125 g (4 oz) lamb's lettuce or
  watercress
1 tablespoon Worcestershire sauce
Tabasco sauce, to taste (optional)

- Heat the olive oil in a large frying pan over a medium heat, then add the mushrooms and cook for 6–7 minutes, stirring frequently, until softened and golden. Stir in the chopped tarragon, chicken and rice and stir to heat through.

- Spoon the rice into serving bowls, scatter over the lamb's lettuce or watercress and drizzle over the Worcestershire sauce. Sprinkle over a little Tabasco, if using, and serve immediately.

20 Grilled Mushroom Breakfast Bowl

Place 8 whole portabellini or small flat field mushrooms on a baking sheet, stalk side up. Scatter over 2 finely chopped garlic cloves and drizzle over 1 tablespoon olive oil. Slide the tray under a preheated grill and cook for 7–8 minutes until tender. Meanwhile, cook 250 g (8 oz) fine green beans in boiling water for 2–3 minutes until just tender and drain. Heat 500 g (1 lb) steamed brown basmati rice, according to the packet instructions. Thickly slice the grilled mushrooms, halve 16 cherry tomatoes and cut the beans into 3.5 cm (1½ inch) lengths. Fold the vegetables into the rice with 1 teaspoon chopped tarragon. Season generously with salt and

pepper and sprinkle over a dash of Worcestershire sauce and a dash of Tabasco sauce, if liked. Serve with lamb's lettuce.

30 Fragrant Brown Rice and Mushroom

Pilau Heat 2 tablespoons groundnut oil in a frying pan over a medium heat. Add 1 finely chopped onion and 2 finely chopped garlic cloves and cook for 5–6 minutes until softened. Add 8 chopped whole portabellini or small flat field mushrooms and cook for 2–3 minutes. Add ¼ teaspoon each of ground cardamom and ground cloves, ½ teaspoon ground cinnamon, 1 teaspoon ground cumin and a generous pinch of saffron threads. Stir in 150 g (5 oz) brown basmati rice and add 650 ml (1 pint 2 fl oz) hot vegetable stock. Simmer gently for 15 minutes, turn off the heat, cover and leave for 5 minutes or until the liquid is absorbed and the rice is tender.

30 Caper and Chorizo Stuffed Chicken Breast with Butter Beans

Serves 4

4 free-range chicken breasts, each about 150 g (5 oz)

1 tablespoon capers, rinsed and drained

175 g (6 oz) roasted red peppers from a jar, drained

8 thin slices lean chorizo

125 g (4 oz) reduced-fat mozzarella, sliced

2 tablespoons chopped flat leaf parsley

1 tablespoon olive oil

200 ml (7 fl oz) dry white wine

2 x 400 g (13 oz) cans butter beans, drained

50 g (2 oz), ready-to-eat, slow-roasted tomatoes (not in oil), chopped

1 small red onion, finely chopped

100 g (3½ oz) rocket leaves

salt and pepper

- Cut the chicken breasts almost in half so that they open into a butterfly shape. Layer the capers, peppers, chorizo and mozzarella over one side of each breast. Sprinkle with parsley and season with salt and pepper. Fold the other side of the breast over the filling, securing with a cocktail stick if necessary.

- Heat the oil in a large, nonstick frying pan over a medium heat and cook the chicken breasts for 2–3 minutes each side until golden. Pour in the white wine and bubble gently for 5–6 minutes or until the chicken is cooked through. Remove from the heat, cover and set aside to rest.

- Meanwhile, toss the butter beans with the slow-roasted tomatoes, red onion and rocket leaves. Season with salt and pepper, then arrange onto serving plates. Cut the chicken in half diagonally and arrange over the bean salad. Serve drizzled with the juices from the pan.

 Chorizo and Butter Bean Salad

Mix together 175 g (6 oz) roasted red peppers from a jar, drained, 2 x 400 g (13 oz) cans butter beans, drained, 1 finely sliced small red onion, 50 g (2 oz) chopped ready-to-eat, slow-roasted tomatoes (not in oil), 4 tablespoons chopped parsley and 50 g (2 oz) roughly chopped chorizo slices. Toss through 100 g (3½ oz) rocket leaves, 1 tablespoon olive oil and 2 tablespoons lemon juice. Season with salt and pepper and serve.

 Toasted Spicy Chicken, Chorizo and Mozzarella Panini Split 4 part-baked baguettes in half lengthways and spread each base with a ½ teaspoon mild harissa paste. Divide 150 g (5 oz) flame-grilled chicken slices, 50 g (2 oz) thinly sliced, lean chorizo, ½ thinly sliced red onion and 125 g (4 oz) sliced reduced-fat mozzarella among the baguettes. Add 100 g (3½ oz) rocket leaves and 2 tablespoons chopped parsley and toast in a panini machine for 3–4 minutes until hot and melted. Alternatively, toast in a nonstick frying pan over a medium-high heat, placing another pan on top of the panini to weight them down. Toast for 2–3 minutes each side until hot and melting. Cut in half and serve.

 # Great Chilled Gazpacho

Serves 4

800 g (1 lb 10 oz) very red, ripe plum tomatoes, roughly chopped
1 small green pepper, cored, deseeded and chopped
1 small red pepper, cored, deseeded and chopped
½ small red onion, chopped
1 garlic clove, finely chopped
½ deseeded cucumber, chopped
100 g (3½ oz) fresh breadcrumbs
2 tablespoons olive oil
150 ml (¼ pint) chilled tomato juice
2 tablespoons aged sherry vinegar
12 ice cubes
salt and pepper
1 tablespoon chopped mint, to garnish

- Put all the ingredients except the sherry vinegar, ice cubes and mint into a food processor or blender and pulse until smooth. Stir in the vinegar and season generously with salt and pepper. Cover with clingfilm and place in the freezer to chill for 10 minutes.

- Place 3 ice cubes in each serving bowl and pour over the chilled soup. Garnish with the chopped mint and serve.

Virgin Bloody Mary Mix together in a large jug 450 ml (¾ pint) tomato juice, 2 teaspoons lemon juice, 1 teaspoon celery salt, ½ teaspoon grated horseradish (optional), a few shakes each of Tabasco and Worcestershire sauce, to taste, and a few grinds of black pepper. Pour into tall glasses filled with crushed ice, garnish each glass with a trimmed celery stick and serve immediately.

Lemony Tomato and Pepper Pasta Heat 1 tablespoon olive oil in a large, nonstick frying pan over a medium heat. Add 1 chopped red onion, 1 small deseeded and chopped green pepper and 1 small deseeded and chopped red pepper and cook, stirring occasionally, for 7–8 minutes until softened. Add 2 finely chopped garlic cloves and cook for a further 2 minutes.

Add 2 x 400 g (13 oz) cans peeled cherry tomatoes, a pinch of sugar, 1 teaspoon finely grated lemon rind, 2 tablespoons sun-dried tomato paste and ½ teaspoon each of chilli flakes and dried oregano. Bring to the boil, reduce the heat to low and simmer gently for 15–18 minutes until fragrant and heated through. Season with salt and pepper and serve tossed through 500 g (1 lb) cooked pasta of your choice.

30 Hot Smoked Trout and Potato Salad

Serves 4

500 g (1 lb) new potatoes
1 tablespoon olive oil
150 g (5 oz) mangetout, trimmed
  and shredded
250 g (8 oz) hot smoked trout
  fillets, flaked
salt and cracked black pepper
lemon wedges, to serve (optional)

Dressing

1 tablespoon horseradish sauce
4 tablespoons reduced-fat crème
  fraîche
1 tablespoon red wine vinegar
1 tablespoon chopped cocktail
  gherkins or cornichons
1 spring onion, sliced
2 tablespoons chopped chives

- Bring a large saucepan of lightly salted water to the boil and cook the new potatoes for 15–18 minutes or until tender.

- Meanwhile, make the dressing. Mix together all the ingredients and season with cracked black pepper.

- Drain the potatoes, then pat dry and toss with the olive oil and a little salt and pepper. Tip into a large, nonstick frying pan over a medium-high heat, and fry for 4–5 minutes, turning frequently, or until golden and crispy.

- Tip the potatoes on to a plate lined with kitchen paper to remove any excess oil, then toss with the mangetout and arrange on serving plates topped with the smoked trout. Drizzle over the dressing, and serve immediately with lemon wedges, if liked, and sliced brown bread on the side.

 **Hot Smoked Trout Pâté** Mash 250 g (8 oz) flaked hot smoked trout fillets with the dressing ingredients as above and season with salt and pepper. Cut ½ deseeded cucumber and 2 celery sticks into batons and toast 4 slices brown bread, then cut diagonally into quarters. To serve, arrange the trout pâté on one large plate or individual plates with the cucumber, celery, pieces of toast and lemon wedges.

 Smoked Trout Salad with Sweet Chilli Dressing Cook 500 g (1 lb) baby new potatoes in lightly salted water for 12–15 minutes until tender. Drain and cool under running cold water. Meanwhile, toss together 250 g (8 oz) flaked hot smoked trout fillets, 200 g (7 oz) crunchy mixed salad leaves, 150 g (5 oz) trimmed and shredded mangetout and 2 finely sliced spring onions. In a separate bowl

mix together 4 tablespoons sweet chilli dipping sauce, 1 tablespoon lime juice and 2 tablespoons chopped coriander. Arrange the potatoes on serving plates and top with the smoked trout salad. Drizzle over the dressing and serve immediately.

Lime and Ginger Coleslaw with 5-Spiced Prawns

Serves 4

½ Chinese cabbage or pointed spring cabbage, thinly shredded
2 carrots, coarsely grated
200 g (7 oz) bean sprouts
1 small bunch of coriander, finely chopped
2 spring onions, thinly sliced
1 tablespoon groundnut oil
250 g (8 oz) shelled, raw jumbo king prawns
2 teaspoons Chinese 5-spice powder
lime wedges, to serve

Dressing

2 teaspoons finely grated fresh root ginger
2 tablespoons lime juice
1 teaspoon palm sugar or soft light brown sugar
2 tablespoons light soy sauce
1 tablespoon groundnut oil

- Toss together in a large bowl the cabbage, carrots, bean sprouts, coriander and spring onions and set aside.

- To make the dressing, mix together all the dressing ingredients in a small bowl and set aside.

- Mix the prawns with the Chinese 5-spice powder until well coated and heat the oil in a nonstick wok or frying pan over a medium-high heat. Add the prawns and toss to cook for 2–3 minutes, or until the prawns are pink and cooked through. Remove from the heat and drain the prawns on kitchen paper to remove any excess oil.

- Toss the dressing with the vegetables and heap the coleslaw on serving plates. Scatter over the prawns and serve with lime wedges.

 Lime and Ginger Prawn Rice Salad Make the dressing as above. Toss together 400 g (13 oz) cooked, peeled prawns with 500 g (1 lb) ready-cooked wild basmati rice, 2 grated carrots and 200 g (7 oz) bean sprouts, then drizzle over the dressing. Sprinkle with 1 small bunch finely chopped coriander and serve immediately.

5-Spice Prawn Skewers Cook 200 g (7 oz) wild basmati rice in lightly salted water for 15–18 minutes until tender, or according to the packet instructions, then drain. Meanwhile, rub 1 tablespoon of Chinese 5-spice paste over 250 g (8 oz) shelled, raw jumbo king prawns and thread on to 4 metal skewers. Place the skewers on a grill rack and slide under a preheated hot grill for 3–4 minutes, turning occasionally, until cooked and slightly charred but still juicy. Prepare the coleslaw and dressing as above, halving the quantities. Arrange the prawn skewers over the hot, drained rice and garnish with lime wedges. Serve with the coleslaw on the side.

30 Tomato and Bread Soup

Serves 4

4 thick slices slightly stale sourdough bread, roughly chopped
250 ml (8 fl oz) skimmed milk
1 kg (2 lb) very ripe plum tomatoes, roughly chopped
4 garlic cloves, roughly chopped
1 large bunch of basil, leaves stripped and roughly chopped
2 tablespoons olive oil
½ cucumber, deseeded and finely diced
½ small red onion, finely chopped
2 teaspoons capers, rinsed and drained
2 teaspoons red wine vinegar
350 ml (12 fl oz) vegetable stock
salt and pepper

- Preheat the oven to 200°C (400°F), Gas Mark 6. Place the bread in a bowl, pour over the milk and set aside.

- Tip the tomatoes into a large roasting tin. Add the garlic, all but 2 tablespoons of the basil and 1 tablespoon of the olive oil and season generously with salt and pepper. Place in the oven for 20–25 minutes or until collapsed and softened.

- Meanwhile, mix together the cucumber, red onion, capers, red wine vinegar, the remaining oil and the 2 tablespoons reserved basil leaves. Season with salt and pepper and set aside.

- Pour the stock into a saucepan and bring to the boil. Squeeze the excess milk from the soaked bread.

- Remove the tomatoes from the oven, stir in the squeezed, soaked bread and enough hot vegetable stock to give the soup a thick, rich texture. Ladle the soup into serving bowls, top each bowl with a spoonful of the cucumber salsa and serve.

Summery Bruschetta with Tomatoes

Toast 4 large slices of sourdough bread on a ridged griddle pan until charred, then rub with the cut edges of 1 garlic clove. Mix together 1 kg (2 lb) roughly chopped ripe plum tomatoes, ½ deseeded and finely chopped cucumber, ½ finely chopped red onion, 2 teaspoons rinsed and drained capers, 2 teaspoons red wine vinegar, 2 tablespoons olive oil and roughly chopped leaves from 1 large bunch of basil. Spoon on to the garlicky toast and serve immediately.

'Panzanella' Tomato and Bread Salad

Lightly toast 4 thick slices of slightly stale sourdough bread and cut into cubes. Mix together 1 kg (2 lb) roughly chopped very ripe plum tomatoes, the roughly chopped leaves from 1 large bunch of basil, ½ finely chopped small red onion, 2 teaspoons rinsed and drained capers, 2 tablespoons olive oil and 2 teaspoons red wine vinegar. Season generously with salt and pepper, then stir in the cubes of toast and set aside for 10–15 minutes for the bread to absorb the juices. Serve with an extra drizzle of olive oil, if desired.

 Smoked Chicken with Beans, Walnuts and Tarragon

Serves 4

200 g (7 oz) fine green beans
1 firm, ripe Hass avocado, stoned and peeled
1 tablespoon lemon juice
175 g (7 oz) mesclun or mixed leaf salad
300 g (10 oz) cooked whole smoked chicken breasts, roughly chopped
1 yellow pepper, finely chopped
50 g (2 oz) walnut pieces
1 shallot, finely chopped (optional)
2 teaspoons chopped tarragon
4 teaspoons walnut oil
salt and pepper
lemon wedges, to serve

- Bring a small saucepan of lightly salted water to the boil and trim the green beans. When the water is boiling add the beans and cook for 3–4 minutes until just tender, then drain and cool under running cold water.

- Meanwhile, dice the flesh of the avocado and toss in the lemon juice to prevent it from turning brown.

- Place the mesclun or mixed leaf salad in a large bowl. Add the chicken, pepper, walnuts, beans and avocado, then gently toss until well combined.

- Heap the salad onto serving plates and sprinkle over the shallot, if using, and tarragon. Season with a little salt and plenty of pepper, then drizzle over the walnut oil. Serve immediately with lemon wedges and nutty granary bread on the side.

 Healthy Chicken and Avocado Baguettes

Mash the flesh from 1 ripe avocado with 1 tablespoon lemon juice and plenty of black pepper, then spread over the base of 4 small, granary baguettes. Slice 300 g (10 oz) cooked whole smoked chicken breasts and layer on top of the avocado. Scatter over 4 teaspoons chopped walnut pieces, 1 finely chopped shallot and 2 teaspoons chopped tarragon, then finish with 175 g (7 oz) mesclun or mixed leaf salad. Drizzle over a little walnut oil and lemon juice, if liked. Cut in half and serve.

 Ricotta and Tarragon Chicken Parcels

Using a sharp knife, cut deep slits along the sides of 4 skinless chicken breasts, about 150 g (5 oz) each, to create 4 pockets. Mix together 125 g (4 oz) ricotta, 25 g (1 oz) chopped walnuts, 2 teaspoons tarragon and 1 finely sliced shallot and season with salt and pepper. Spoon the ricotta mixture into the pockets, then wrap each breast in a large slice of Parma ham. Heat 1 tablespoon olive oil in a nonstick frying pan over a medium-high heat and pan-fry for 4–5 minutes each side until almost cooked through. Add 125 ml (4 fl oz) dry white wine to the pan and simmer for 2–3 minutes or until the chicken is cooked. Meanwhile, cook 200 g (7 oz) trimmed fine green beans in boiling water for 3–4 minutes or until just tender. Cool under running cold water. Remove the chicken from the heat and cut into thick slices. To assemble, arrange the chicken over the cooked green beans on serving plates. Serve with a mesclun salad dressed in walnut oil, if liked, and lemon wedges.

10 Real Guacamole with Raw Vegetables

Serves 4

2 large, firm, ripe avocados
½ small red onion
2 tablespoons lime juice
3 tablespoons finely chopped coriander
¼ teaspoon garlic powder
¼ teaspoon celery salt
pinch of cayenne
½ teaspoon paprika
3 tomatoes
few dashes of Tabasco (optional)
salt and pepper

To serve

350 g (11½ oz) carrots, cut into batons
350 g (11½ oz) cauliflower florets
4 celery sticks, cut into batons
250 g (8 oz) radishes, trimmed
125 g (4 oz) baby sweetcorn

- Peel the avocados and remove the stones, then mash the flesh in a small bowl with the back of a fork or potato masher to break it up.

- Finely chop the red onion and add to the avocado along with the lime juice, coriander, garlic powder, celery salt and spices. Mix until almost smooth, with some small lumps, then season with salt and pepper.

- Quarter, deseed and finely chop the tomatoes, then stir them into the avocado mixture. Add the Tabasco, if using.

- Scoop into a serving bowl and arrange on a platter with the selection of raw vegetables.

20 Avocado and Crab Meat Salad

Combine together in a bowl 300 g (10 oz) cooked white crab meat, the finely grated rind and juice of 1 lime, 1 finely chopped shallot, 3 tablespoons chopped coriander, 1 deseeded and finely chopped red chilli and ½ small deseeded and finely chopped cucumber. Cut 2 large, firm, ripe avocados in half and remove the stones. Spoon the crab salad into the avocado halves and serve with slices of lightly buttered brown bread.

30 Steak Wraps with Chunky Guacamole

Rub a 400 g (13 oz) lean rump steak with 1 tablespoon olive oil and 1 tablespoon spicy Cajun seasoning mix. Heat a ridged griddle pan over a medium-high heat and cook the steak, turning occasionally, for 4–5 minutes or until nicely charred and almost cooked but still pink. Remove the steak from the heat and set aside to rest. Meanwhile, dice the flesh of 2 large, firm, ripe avocados and toss gently with

the guacamole ingredients, as above. Scatter 4 large, warmed multiseed bread wraps with ½ shredded iceberg lettuce and 1 deseeded and thinly sliced red pepper. Slice the steak thinly and arrange over the salad. Spoon over the guacamole, then roll up the wraps tightly. Cut in half and serve immediately with a few dashes of Tabasco sprinkled over, if liked.

 # Mixed Rice and Bean Salad with Smoked Duck Breast

Serves 4

175 g (6 oz) basmati and wild rice mix, rinsed in cold water

1 green pepper, cored, deseeded and diced

1 small mango, peeled, stoned and diced

1 large bunch of coriander

2 spring onions, finely sliced (optional)

400 g (13 oz) can adzuki beans, drained

4 tablespoons lime juice

350 g (11½ oz) smoked duck breast, trimmed of excess fat and sliced

handful of alfalfa shoots

salt and pepper

lime wedges, to serve

- Bring 500 ml (17 fl oz) lightly salted water to the boil, tip in the rice and cook for 15–18 minutes until the rice is tender, or according to the packet instructions. Drain into a colander and cool quickly under running cold water.

- Meanwhile, mix together the pepper, mango, coriander, spring onions, if using, adzuki beans and lime juice in a large bowl.

- Fold the cooled rice into the adzuki bean salad and divide into deep serving bowls. Arrange the slices of duck breast over the salad, then top with the alfalfa sprouts. Serve immediately with lime wedges on the side.

 Quick Bean, Rice and Tuna Salad

Mix together in a large bowl 500 g (1 lb) cooked wild and basmati rice, 1 deseeded and diced green pepper, 1 small diced cucumber, 1 chopped large bunch coriander, 400 g (13 oz) can adzuki beans, drained, 4 tablespoons lime juice and 2 finely sliced spring onions, if liked. Season with salt and pepper, then divide into serving bowls. Top with 350 g (11½ oz) flaked smoked tuna, and serve.

Pan-Fried Duck Breast with Adzuki Rice Mix and Mango Salsa

Cook 175 g (6 oz) basmati and wild rice mix in 500 ml (17 fl oz) lightly salted water for 15–18 minutes until the rice is tender, or according to the packet instructions. Meanwhile, make a salsa by mixing together 1 deseeded and diced yellow pepper, the diced flesh of 1 mango, 1 chopped large bunch of coriander and 2 finely sliced spring onions. Stir in 2 tablespoons lime juice and 1 tablespoon vegetable oil and set aside. Heat another tablespoon of

vegetable oil in a large, nonstick frying pan over a medium-high heat and pan-fry 450 g (14½ oz) duck mini fillets for 4–6 minutes until cooked, turning occasionally. Remove the duck from the heat and set aside to rest for 2–3 minutes. Tip a 400 g (13 oz) can adzuki beans into a sieve and drain the cooked rice directly over the beans to heat the beans. Drain well, then spoon on to serving plates. Cut the duck fillets into slices and arrange them over the bean and rice mix. Serve immediately with the salsa and lime wedges on the side.

Roasted Peppers on Rye

Serves 4

8 slices seeded rye bread or multigrain bread
1 garlic clove, halved (optional)
175 g (6 oz) flame-roasted red peppers, drained and sliced
2 tablespoons toasted pine nuts
100 g (3½ oz) reduced-fat feta cheese (optional)

Artichoke paste

400 g (13 oz) can artichokes in water, drained
125 g (4 oz) ricotta or extra-light cream cheese
1 tablespoon lemon juice
salt and pepper

- Heat a ridged griddle pan over a high heat and toast the sliced bread for 1–2 minutes each side until toasted and lightly charred. Rub the toast with the cut edges of the garlic clove, if liked.

- To make the artichoke paste, put the artichokes in the small bowl of a food processor or blender and pulse until roughly chopped and textured. Add the ricotta and lemon juice and pulse to a paste. Season with salt and pepper.

- Spread the artichoke paste over the slices of toast and top the paste with the roasted peppers. Sprinkle over the toasted pine nuts, crumble over the feta, if using, and serve.

 Pepper, Artichoke and Spinach Pizzas

Make the artichoke paste as above, and spread over 2 large ready-made pizza bases. Scatter over 100 g (3½ oz) baby leaf spinach and top with a 280 g (9 oz) jar well-drained, mixed, sliced peppers. Crumble over 100 g (3½ oz) reduced-fat feta cheese and sprinkle with 2 tablespoons toasted pine nuts. Place in a preheated oven, 220°C (425°F), Gas Mark 7, for 10–12 minutes until the pizzas are crisp.

 Spicy Bulgar Wheat and Roast Peppers

Bring 500 ml (17 fl oz) vegetable stock to the boil in a large saucepan. Add 250 g (8 oz) bulgar wheat and cook for 7 minutes. Turn off the heat, cover and leave for 12–15 minutes until the liquid is absorbed and the grains are tender. Meanwhile, fry 1 chopped red onion and 2 chopped garlic cloves in 1 tablespoon olive oil for 5–6 minutes until softened, stirring occasionally. Add 200 g (7 oz) chopped mushrooms and cook for 2–3 minutes until tender, then add 400 g (13 oz) can artichokes in water, drained and roughly chopped, 175 g (6 oz) chopped roasted peppers, 2 tablespoons lemon juice and 1 small bunch of chopped coriander. Fold through the bulgar wheat. Serve topped with dollops of fat-free Greek yogurt and lemon wedges for squeezing.

 # Fragrant Soba Noodle Soup

Serves 4

1 lemon grass stalk, leaves stripped

1.2 litres (2 pints) clear chicken or vegetable stock

2.5 cm (1 inch) piece of fresh root ginger, finely chopped

3 lime leaves, thinly sliced

1 small red chilli, deseeded and finely sliced (optional)

1 tablespoon fish sauce

250 g (8 oz) buckwheat soba noodles

200 g (7 oz) firm tofu, diced

1 spring onion, thinly sliced

2 tablespoons chopped coriander leaves

- Finely slice the tender hearts of the lemon grass stalks and place in a saucepan with the chicken stock, ginger, lime leaves, chilli, if using, and fish sauce. Bring to the boil, then reduce the heat to low and simmer gently for 10–12 minutes.

- Meanwhile, bring a large saucepan of water to the boil and cook the noodles for 6–7 minutes until tender, or according to the packet instructions. Drain the noodles and divide among 4 warmed bowls.

- Scatter the tofu over the noodles and then carefully ladle over the hot, fragrant soup. Scatter over the spring onions and coriander and serve immediately.

 Mixed Noodle and Chicken Thai Broth

Cook 250 g (8 oz) buckwheat soba noodles as above, and heat 350 g (11½ oz) cooked medium egg noodles according to the packet instructions. Meanwhile, heat 1.2 litres (2 pints) chicken stock in a saucepan with 1 teaspoon each of minced lemon grass, ginger and Thai red chilli paste (nam prik pao) and simmer for 3–4 minutes. Divide the noodles between 4 deep bowls and scatter over 300 g (10 oz) diced, cooked chicken. Ladle over the hot broth and serve with 1 sliced spring onion and chopped coriander leaves.

 Chicken and Soba Noodle Salad

Cook 250 g (8 oz) buckwheat soba noodles in boiling water or 1.2 litres (2 pints) clear chicken stock for 6–7 minutes or until tender. Drain and cool under running cold water. Meanwhile, put 1 lemon grass stalk, leaves stripped and roughly chopped, 2.5 cm (1 inch) peeled and finely chopped fresh root ginger and 1 deseeded and roughly chopped small red chilli in a mini chopper. Add 2 tablespoons groundnut oil and 4 tablespoons lime juice, then blend until smooth. Toss the cooked noodles in the lemon grass dressing and set aside.

Shred 200 g (13 oz) cooked chicken into a separate bowl, then mix in 200 g (7 oz) diced firm tofu and 125 g (4 oz) shredded mangetout. Tip in the dressed noodles and toss gently to combine. Pile the noodle salad on serving plates, scatter over 1 thinly sliced spring onion, 2 tablespoons chopped coriander and 2 tablespoons chopped blanched peanuts and serve.

QuickCook
Fish and Shellfish

Recipes listed by cooking time

30

2

10

 # Pan-Fried Salmon with Mixed Bean Salad

Serves 4

1 tablespoon extra virgin rapeseed oil

4 tail end salmon fillets, about 150 g (5 oz) each

cracked black pepper

Mixed bean salad

2 x 400 g (13 oz) can mixed beans, drained

½ tablespoon extra virgin rapeseed oil

1 tablespoon red wine vinegar

2 tablespoons finely chopped mint

75 g (3 oz) rocket leaves

salt

- Season the salmon fillets with cracked black pepper, then place under a preheated grill for 2–3 minutes until golden and crispy. Turn the fillets over and grill for a further 2–3 minutes until almost cooked.

- Meanwhile, to make the mixed bean salad, put the mixed beans, the oil, vinegar and mint in a large bowl and mix to combine. Season with salt and pepper, then toss through the rocket leaves.

- Transfer the mixed bean salad to serving plates, top with the salmon fillets and serve.

 Baked Salmon and Mixed Beans

Prepare the mixed bean salad as above, omitting the rocket. Divide the bean salad among 4 large pieces of baking parchment and top each mound of beans with a tail end salmon fillet, about 150 g (5 oz) each. Fold the edges of the paper over the beans and salmon to make 4 sealed parcels. Place the parcels on a large baking sheet and put in a preheated oven, 200°C (400°F), Gas Mark 6, for 12–15 minutes or until the fish is cooked and the beans are hot. Serve with rocket leaves.

 Salmon, Bean and Couscous Salad

Season 4 chunky salmon fillets, about 150 g (5 oz) each, with cracked black pepper. Heat 1 tablespoon extra virgin rapeseed oil over a medium heat, then pan-fry the fillets for 7–8 minutes until cooked through, turning once. Set aside to cool, then flake the fillets into large pieces. Pour 225 ml (7½ fl oz) boiling water over 125 g (4 oz) lemon and coriander couscous and leave to stand for 5 minutes until the liquid is absorbed and the grains are

tender. Add to the couscous 400 g (13 oz) can mixed beans, drained, 2 tablespoons chopped mint, 2 sliced spring onions, 2 tablespoons lemon juice and ½ tablespoon extra virgin rapeseed oil and season generously with salt and pepper. Bring a small saucepan of water to the boil and cook 200 g (7 oz) trimmed asparagus tips for 2–3 minutes until just tender. Drain and cool under running cold water. Toss the asparagus with the mix bean and couscous salad and serve topped with the flaked salmon.

LOW-FISH-XYV

30 Hot and Sour Prawn Soup

Serves 4

1 litre (1¾ pints) light and clear chicken or vegetable stock

3 tablespoons Thai fish sauce

1 tablespoon rice wine vinegar

1 tablespoon lime juice

1 tablespoon palm sugar or soft light brown sugar

1 garlic clove, sliced

1 red chilli, sliced thinly

3 kaffir lime leaves

2 teaspoons tamarind paste

200 g (7 oz) rice vermicelli

125 g (4 oz) baby corn, sliced

250 g (8 oz) raw peeled tiger prawns

100 g (3½ oz) bean sprouts

2 tablespoons shredded mint

- Pour the stock into a large saucepan and add the fish sauce, vinegar, lime juice, sugar, garlic, chilli, lime leaves and tamarind paste. Bring to the boil over a medium-high heat, then reduce the heat and simmer gently for 12 minutes.

- Meanwhile, put the rice vermicelli in a bowl of boiling water for 2–3 minutes until tender, or cook according to the packet instructions. Drain well and divide among warmed deep serving bowls.

- Stir the baby corn into the broth and simmer for 2 minutes, then add the prawns and simmer for a further 2–3 minutes until the prawns are just cooked.

- Ladle the broth into the bowls of vermicelli, then scatter over the bean sprouts and mint and serve immediately.

Thai Prawn and Coconut Soup

Bring 500 ml (17 fl oz) chicken stock to the boil. Stir in 4 tablespoons Thai tom yum paste, 2 tablespoons lime juice, 3 kaffir lime leaves and 1 teaspoon fish sauce, reduce the heat and simmer for 4–5 minutes. Cook 200 g (7 oz) rice vermicelli as above, then divide among 4 deep bowls. Stir 125 g (4 oz) sliced baby corn and 250 g (8 oz) raw peeled tiger prawns into the soup and simmer for 2–3 minutes until the prawns are cooked. Add 200 ml (7 fl oz) reduced-fat coconut milk and bring to the boil. Ladle over the vermicelli and serve.

Hot and Sour Prawn Stir-Fry

Mix together in a small bowl 2 tablespoons fish sauce, 1 tablespoon each of rice wine vinegar and lime juice, 1 tablespoon palm sugar or soft light brown sugar and 2 teaspoons tamarind paste. Heat 1 tablespoon groundnut oil in a hot wok over a medium-high heat and stir-fry 2 sliced garlic cloves, 1 thinly sliced red chilli (deseed for less heat), 1 tablespoon chopped fresh root ginger and 1 sliced shallot for 30 seconds. Tip in 250 g (8 oz) raw peeled tiger prawns and stir-fry for 2–3 minutes until just

cooked through. Turn off the heat, pour over the dressing mixture and set aside to cool. Meanwhile, cook 200 g (7 oz) rice vermicelli as above, then cool in ice-cold water. When ready to serve, drain the vermicelli and toss with the cooled prawn mixture, 100 g (3½ oz) bean sprouts and 2 tablespoons shredded mint. Serve with lime wedges on the side.

LOW-FISH-VAJ

 # Grilled Sardines with Mango and Lime Salsa

Serves 4

1 teaspoon finely grated fresh root ginger

finely grated rind and juice of 1 lime

1 small bunch of coriander, roughly chopped

1 tablespoon groundnut oil

½ large red chilli, deseeded and chopped

12–16 fresh sardines, scaled, gutted and cleaned

Mango and lime salsa

1 firm, ripe mango, peeled, stoned and diced

4 tomatoes, deseeded and diced

1 spring onion, finely chopped

2 tablespoons lime juice

½ large red chilli, deseeded and chopped

- Place the ginger, lime zest and juice, coriander, oil and half the chilli in a mini chopper and blend to make a rough paste. Alternatively, use a pestle and mortar.

- Score small slits into the sardine flesh, then rub the paste all over, massaging it into the slits.

- Place the sardines onto a grill rack and slide under a hot preheated grill for 4–5 minutes or until cooked and slightly blackened, turning once.

- Meanwhile, make the salsa by combining all the ingredients in a small bowl and mixing well.

- Serve the sardines straight off the grill with the salsa.

 Sardines on Toast with Mango and Lime Salsa Make the salsa as above and grill 4 large slices of bread. Arrange 300 g (10 oz) canned sardines in hot chilli or piri-piri on the toasted bread and serve with the salsa.

Grilled Sardines with Cumin Potatoes and Mango and Lime Salsa Tip 500 g (1 lb) small new potatoes into a large saucepan with 1 tablespoon olive oil, some coarse sea salt and 1–2 teaspoon cumin seeds, to taste. Cook for 20–25 minutes, shaking the pan frequently, until golden and crispy. Meanwhile, place 1 teaspoon finely grated fresh root ginger, the finely grated rind and juice of 1 lime, 1 small

roughly chopped bunch of coriander, 1 tablespoon groundnut oil and ½ large deseeded and chopped red chilli in a mini chopper or pestle and mortar and grind to a rough paste. Rub the prepared paste all over 12–16 scaled, gutted and cleaned fresh sardines. Place the sardines on a grill rack under a preheated grill for 8–10 minutes until golden and cooked, turning once. Serve with the cumin potatoes and the mango and lime salsa, as above.

LOW-FISH-GYD

10 Spicy Seafood Salad

Serves 4

1 teaspoon caster sugar
2 tablespoons mirin
1 tablespoon light soy sauce
1 small red chilli, deseeded and finely chopped
2 tablespoons lime juice
350 g (11½ oz) medium egg noodles
400 g (13 oz) cooked fruits de mer or seafood selection
lime wedges, to serve

- Place the sugar, mirin, soy sauce, chilli and lime juice in a small saucepan over a medium-low heat and stir until the sugar has dissolved. Pour the dressing into a jug or bowl and set aside for the flavours to develop.

- Meanwhile, cook the noodles in a large saucepan of boiling water for 2–3 minutes until tender, or according to the packet instructions, then cool under running cold water and drain well.

- Tip the fruits de mer or seafood selection into a large bowl. Add the noodles and dressing and toss until the seafood and noodles are well coated in the dressing. Serve immediately with lime wedges.

20 Chilli Seafood Linguine

Cook 400 g (13 oz) linguine in a saucepan of salted boiling water, according the packet instructions. Meanwhile, heat 1 tablespoon olive oil in a nonstick frying pan over a medium heat, and add 1 small deseeded and chopped red chilli, 2 finely chopped garlic cloves and 2 finely sliced spring onions. Cook gently for 2–3 minutes, then add 250 g (8 oz) halved cherry tomatoes and 3 tablespoons lime juice. Season generously with salt and pepper, then tip in 400 g (13 oz) cooked fruits de mer or seafood selection and stir-fry for 1 minute to reheat. Remove from the heat, tip in the drained linguine and toss until well combined. Serve immediately.

30 Seafood Risotto

Pour 900 ml (1½ pints) vegetable stock into a saucepan and bring up to a gentle boil. Meanwhile, heat 1 tablespoon olive oil in a large frying pan over a medium heat, add 2 chopped shallots and cook for 4–5 minutes until softened, then add 300 g (10 oz) risotto rice and stir for a minute, or until the grains are well coated and look translucent. Add 75 ml (3 fl oz) dry vermouth, then simmer rapidly until absorbed, stirring constantly. Stirring and simmering constantly, take 17 minutes to incorporate the boiling vegetable stock, a ladleful at a time, or until the rice is 'al dente'. When the risotto is cooked, stir in 2 teaspoons

grated lemon rind, 400 g (13 oz) cooked fruits de mer or seafood selection and season with salt and pepper. Stir until the seafood is heated through, then spoon into deep bowls and serve.

 Baked Sea Bream with Cumin and Cucumber Yogurt

Serves 4

2 garlic cloves, finely chopped
2 tablespoons chopped parsley
finely grated rind 1 lemon
¼ teaspoon chilli flakes (optional)
1 teaspoon cumin seeds, crushed
1 tablespoon olive oil
4 sea bream fillets, about 150 g
  (5 oz) each, pin-boned
50 ml (2 fl oz) dry white wine
lemon wedges, to serve
salt and pepper

Cumin and cucumber yogurt

1 teaspoon cumin seeds, crushed
½ small cucumber 6 tablespoons
  fat-free natural yogurt
2 teaspoons lemon juice

- Preheat the oven to 220 °C (425 °F), Gas Mark 7. Mix together the garlic, parsley, lemon rind, chilli flakes, and the cumin seeds in a small bowl. Stir in the olive oil and rub the mixture over the sea bream fillets.

- Put the fillets in a foil-lined raosting tin and pour over the white wine. Season with salt and pepper and cover with foil, sealing tightly. Place in the oven and bake for about 8 minutes, or until the fish is just cooked through.

- Meanwhile make the cumin and cucumber yogurt. Heat a small frying pan over a medium heat, then add the cumin seeds and dry roast until they begin to smell fragrant. Deseed and finely chop the cucumber, tip into a bowl, mix with the yogurt and lemon juice, and season.

- Remove the sea bream from the oven and serve immediately drizzled with any juices from the roasting pan, alongside steamed basmati rice, the cumin and cucumber yogurt and poppadums on the side.

 Sea Bream with Cumin-Scented Yogurt Pin-bone 4 sea bream fillets, 150 g (5 oz) each, and season with salt and pepper. Heat 1 tablespoon olive oil in a large frying pan over a medium heat, then add the fillets, skin side down, and pan-fry for 3–4 minutes until crisp. Turn and cook for 2–3 more minutes until cooked through. Meanwhile, mix ½ teaspoon ground cumin, 6 tablespoons fat-free natural yogurt, 2 teaspoons lemon juice and 2 tablespoons chopped parsley and season. Serve with the fish and steamed rice.

 Baked Sea Bream and Spinach Parcels Ask the fishmonger to fillet 4 small sea bream. Mix together 2 finely chopped garlic cloves, 2 tablespoons chopped parsley, the finely grated rind of 1 lemon and 2 teaspoons cumin seeds with 200 g (7 oz) baby leaf spinach in a large frying pan over a medium heat until the spinach is just wilted. Place 1 fillet from each sea bream on a foil-lined baking sheet, skin side down. Top each fillet with one-quarter of the wilted spinach, then cover with the corresponding fillet,

skin side up this time, to form 4 parcels. Secure each parcel with cocktail sticks or tie with string. Bake in a preheated oven, 220 °C (425 °F), Gas Mark 7, for about 15 minutes, until cooked through and the flesh flakes easily when pressed in the centre with a knife. Serve with steamed brown basmati rice and the cumin and cucumber yogurt as above.

 # Soy and Ginger Tuna Fishcakes

Serves 4

450 g (14½ oz) tuna steak, roughly chopped
2 tablespoons sweet soy sauce or ketjap manis
2 teaspoons finely grated fresh root ginger
1 long shallot, finely chopped
2 tablespoons beaten egg
150 g (5 oz) panko or coarse, crisp breadcrumbs
groundnut oil, for greasing
sweet chilli dipping sauce, to serve

Soy dipping sauce

2 tablespoons dark soy sauce
2 tablespoons mirin
2 tablespoons sake
2 teaspoons finely grated fresh root ginger

- Preheat the oven to 200°C (400°F), Gas Mark 6. To make the soy dipping sauce, put all the ingredients in a small saucepan over a medium-high heat and bring up to boiling point. Reduce the heat and simmer for 2–3 minutes, pour the sauce into a shallow serving dish and set aside to cool.

- Meanwhile, place the tuna in the bowl of a food processor or blender with the sweet soy sauce or ketjap manis, ginger, shallot and egg. Pulse quickly to just combine, then stir in 50 g (2 oz) of the panko or breadcrumbs. Form the mixture into 8 small fishcakes and coat each one well in the remaining breadcrumbs.

- Place the fishcakes on a lightly greased, nonstick baking sheet and bake in the oven for 15 minutes, or until crisp and golden, turning once.

- Once the fishcakes are cooked, arrange them on serving plates with the soy dipping sauce and sweet chilli dipping sauce served separately.

 Quick Tuna Fishcakes

Mix a 400 g (13 oz) can tuna in brine, drained, with 4 teaspoons finely grated ginger, 2 beaten eggs and 50 g (2 oz) panko or coarse, crisp breadcrumbs. Form into 4 large, flattened fishcakes. Coat in another 50 g (2 oz) panko or coarse, crisp breadcrumbs. Heat 1 tablespoon groundnut oil in a frying pan over a medium heat, then pan-fry the fishcakes for 4–5 minutes or until crisp, turning once. Serve with sweet chilli dipping sauce on the side.

 Tuna Rösti

Coarsely grate 2 large potatoes and 2 carrots. Place in a sieve over the sink and squeeze out any excess moisture. Flake 100 g (3½ oz) can of tuna in brine, drained, into a large bowl and mix with 1 small, beaten egg, 2 tablespoons chopped coriander and the grated vegetables. Heat 1 tablespoon groundnut oil in a large, nonstick frying pan over a medium heat, then scrape the tuna and potato mixture into the pan to make 1 large rösti. Cook for about

4 minutes or until crisp and golden, then flip over and cook for a further 3–4 minutes. Carefully remove to a plate lined with kitchen paper to drain off any excess fat. Serve in wedges with the soy dipping sauce, as above, and sweet chilli dipping sauce.

Cajun-Spiced Tiger Prawns with Mixed Rice

Serves 4

300 g (10 oz) long grain wild rice
400 g (13 oz) raw peeled tiger or jumbo king prawns
1 large red pepper, thinly sliced
1 red onion, cut into thin wedges

Cajun spice mix

1 teaspoon cayenne pepper
1 teaspoon paprika
1 teaspoon dried thyme
1 teaspoon dried oregano
½ teaspoon dried onion granules
½ teaspoon dried garlic granules
½ teaspoon ground cumin
½ teaspoon sea salt
½ teaspoon black pepper

To serve

rocket leaves
lime wedges
griddled flour tortillas (optional)

- Bring a large saucepan of salted water to the boil and cook the rice for 15–18 minutes, or according to the packet instructions.

- Meanwhile, combine the Cajun spice mix ingredients in a large bowl, add the prawns and toss until well coated with the spices. Lay the pepper and onion on a small baking tray and place under a preheated grill for 4–5 minutes until beginning to lightly char.

- Remove the tray from under the grill and use tongs to turn over the vegetables. Arrange the prawns in a single layer on a separate small baking tray and place both trays under the grill for a further 4–5 minutes, turning the prawns once. The prawns should be cooked through but still juicy and the peppers and onions should be slightly charred but still firm.

- Drain the rice thoroughly and spoon on to serving plates. Scatter the peppers and onions over the rice, arrange the prawns on top and serve immediately with rocket leaves, lime wedges and griddled flour tortillas, if desired.

 Quick Spiced Prawn Rice Salad

Take 500 g (1 lb) ready-cooked rice, but do not heat. Tip the rice into a large bowl and add 1 thinly sliced red pepper and 1 red onion, cut into very thin wedges. In a separate bowl toss 400 g (13 oz) cooked peeled king prawns with 1½ tablespoons ready-made Cajun seasoning. Heat 1 tablespoon vegetable oil in a frying pan over a high heat, add the prawns and fry for 1 minute to heat through. Scatter over the salad and serve.

 Quick Cajun Prawn Rice

Heat 500 g (1 lb) ready-cooked wild basmati rice according to the packet instructions. Heat 1 tablespoon vegetable oil in a nonstick frying pan over a medium heat, then add 1 small, thinly sliced red onion and 1 deseeded and thinly sliced pepper and cook, stirring occasionally, for 6–7 minutes or until softened and golden. Meanwhile, make the Cajun spice mix as above, then add 400 g

(13 oz) raw peeled tiger or jumbo king prawns and toss until the prawns are well coated in the mix. Tip the prawns into the pan with the vegetables for a further 3–4 minutes until the prawns are pink and cooked through. Toss with the hot rice and serve in bowls with rocket leaves, lime wedges and tortillas, as above.

10 Swordfish Steaks with Basil and Pinenut Oil

Serves 4

1 teaspoon extra virgin
  rapeseed oil
4 swordfish steaks, about
  150 g (5 oz) each
250 g (8 oz) herby baby leaf salad
75 g (3 oz) ready-to-eat,
  slow-roasted tomatoes,
  roughly chopped
salt and pepper

Basil and pinenut oil

1 small bunch of basil, leaves
  stripped
5 teaspoons extra virgin
  rapeseed oil
1 tablespoon toasted pine nuts
1 tablespoon lemon juice

- Rub the oil over the swordfish steaks and season generously with salt and pepper. Place on a preheated ridged griddle pan over a medium heat and cook for 5–7 minutes, turning once, until the fish is nicely charred but still slightly rare.

- Meanwhile, to make the basil oil, put all the ingredients in a mini chopper or in a small food processor bowl and pulse to blend to a smooth paste. Season the basil oil with salt and pepper, then scrape into a small bowl. Alternatively, crush in a pestle and mortar.

- Pile the baby leaf salad on to serving plates and scatter with the slow-roasted tomatoes. Serve alongside the griddled swordfish, with a little basil and pinenut oil drizzled over each.

---

2 **Griddled Swordfish with Basil-Dressed Warm Potato Salad** Cook 350 g (11½ oz) baby new potatoes in a saucepan of salted boiling water for 15–18 minutes until tender. Meanwhile, make the basil and pinenut oil as above, and griddle 4 swordfish steaks, about 150 g (5 oz) each, as above. While the swordfish is grilling, cook 200 g (7 oz) green beans for 3–4 minutes until tender but still firm, then drain and place in a bowl with 75 g (3 oz) roughly chopped ready-to-eat, slow-roasted tomatoes, 2 sliced spring onions and 75 g (3 oz)

pitted black olives. Slice the swordfish steaks thickly. Drain the potatoes and toss with the tomatoes and beans and half of the basil and pinenut oil. Transfer the vegetables to serving plates, then top with the swordfish. Serve drizzled with the remaining basil and pinenut oil.

3 **Pan-Fried Tuna Marinated in Basil-Infused Oil** Put the leaves from 1 small bunch of basil and 5 teaspoons extra virgin rapeseed oil into a mini chopper and blend until smooth. Season with salt and pepper, then rub half of the oil over a 625 g (1¼ lb) tuna loin and leave to marinate for 10 minutes. Heat a frying pan over a medium heat, then pan-fry the tuna for 10–12 minutes until seared all over, turning frequently. Remove from the pan and slice thinly. Serve with a herby baby leaf salad sprinkled with toasted pine nuts, and the remaining basil oil.

 # Red Mullet with Capers and a Warm Tomato Salad

Serves 4

8 red mullet fillets, about 100 g (3½ oz) each, scaled and gutted

finely grated rind of 1 lemon, plus 2 tablespoons juice

2 teaspoons baby capers, rinsed and drained

2 spring onions, finely sliced

375 g (12 oz) mixed red and yellow cherry tomatoes

150 g (5 oz) fine green beans, trimmed

2 garlic cloves, finely chopped

50 g (2 oz) can anchovies, drained and chopped

1 tablespoon olive oil

2 tablespoons chopped parsley

salt and pepper

8 caperberries, to garnish

- Preheat the oven to 200°C (400°F), Gas Mark 6. Tear off four large sheets of foil and line with baking parchment. Place 2 red mullet fillets on each piece of baking parchment, then scatter over the lemon rind, capers and spring onions and season with salt and pepper. Fold over the paper-lined foil and scrunch the edges together to seal. Place the parcels on a large baking sheet.

- Put the cherry tomatoes in an ovenproof dish with the green beans, garlic, anchovies, oil and lemon juice. Season with salt and pepper and mix well.

- Bake the vegetables in the oven for 10 minutes until tender. Place the fish next to the vegetables in the oven and bake for 8–10 minutes until the flesh flakes easily when pressed in the centre with a knife.

- Remove the fish and vegetables from the oven. Spoon the vegetables on to warmed plates, then top with the steamed red mullet. Sprinkle over the chopped parsley, garnish with the caperberries and serve immediately with slices of sourdough bread.

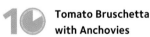

Tomato Bruschetta with Anchovies Heat a griddle pan and grill 4 slices of sourdough bread for 2–3 minutes until nicely charred on both sides. Halve 375 g (12 oz) red and yellow cherry tomatoes and toss with 8 capers, 2 finely sliced spring onions, 2 tablespoons chopped parsley and 1 tablespoon each of olive oil and aged sherry vinegar. Spoon the tomatoes over the bread. Top with 300 g (10 oz) anchovy fillets. Serve.

Sun-Dried Tomato and Caper-Marinated Red Mullet Score several shallow slits into the skin of 8 scaled and gutted red mullet fillets, about 100 g (3½ oz) each, and place them in an ovenproof dish. Mix together 2 tablespoons sun-dried tomato paste, 1 tablespoon caper paste (or 1 tablespoon rinsed capers, very finely chopped, if paste is unavailable), the finely grated rind of 1 lemon, 1 tablespoon olive oil, 1 finely chopped garlic clove, 2 tablespoons chopped parsley and 25 g (1 oz) can finely chopped drained anchovies. Rub the mixture over the red mullet fillets and set aside to marinate for about 10 minutes. Roast in a preheated oven, 200°C (400°F), Gas Mark 6, for about 10 minutes or until the flesh flakes easily when pressed in the centre with a knife. Serve with steamed couscous and scattered with 75 g (3 oz) anchovy-stuffed olives.

20 Aromatic Steamed Mussels

Serves 4

1 tablespoon groundnut oil

2 shallots, thinly sliced

1 red chilli, deseeded and finely sliced

2.5 cm (1 inch) piece of fresh root ginger, peeled and finely chopped

1 garlic clove, finely sliced

3 tablespoons Pernod

350 ml (12 fl oz) fish or vegetable stock

1 small preserved lemon, finely chopped

1.5 kg (3 lb) mussels, scrubbed and debearded

1 small bunch of coriander, roughly chopped

salt and pepper

- Heat the oil in a large, heavy-based casserole over a medium-low heat, then stir in the shallots, chilli, ginger and garlic and cook gently for 7–8 minutes or until softened, stirring occasionally. Add the Pernod to the pan and simmer to evaporate, then add the stock and preserved lemon and bring up to boiling point.

- Tip in the mussels, discarding any that won't close. Season with salt and pepper, then stir the mussels to coat them in the shallot mix. Cover the casserole with a tight-fitting lid and steam gently, shaking the pan occasionally, for 4–5 minutes until the mussels are cooked. Part way through cooking, use a large metal spoon to stir the mussels thoroughly, lifting the ones from the bottom of the pan to the top. Replace the lid for the remaining cooking time until the mussels have opened, discarding any that remain closed.

- Heap the mussels into deep bowls, scatter over the coriander and serve immediately with a large bowl to the side for the empty shells.

---

10 Thai Pan-Fried Mussels
Heat 1 tablespoon groundnut oil in a frying pan over a medium heat, then add 2 thinly sliced shallots, ½ teaspoon minced chilli from a jar, 1 teaspoon each finely chopped lemon grass, finely chopped ginger and ½ teaspoon finely chopped garlic. Cook gently for 3 minutes, then add 400 ml (14 fl oz) reduced-fat coconut milk. Simmer for 2 minutes, then stir in 400 g (13 oz) cooked, shelled mussels and the coriander. Bring to the boil and serve with rice.

30 Grilled Mussels Topped with Herbed Breadcrumbs Cook 1.5 kg (3 lb) mussels, scrubbed and debearded as above. Remove one side from each mussel shell, discarding the empty half shells. Break in two any empty whole shells, discarding one half and sitting any loose mussels from the base of the pan inside the other half. Mix 75 g (3 oz) coarse breadcrumbs with the finely grated rind of 1 lemon and 1 large bunch of chopped coriander. Arrange the shells on a large baking sheet and scatter the breadcrumbs over the mussels. Lightly spray the breadcrumbs with light olive oil and slide under a preheated grill for 2–3 minutes until crisp. Serve with a salad of mixed leaves.

30 Baked Salmon Fillets with Ginger and Chillies

Serves 4

2.5 cm (1 inch) piece of fresh root ginger, finely chopped

1 green chilli, deseeded and finely sliced

3 tablespoons chopped coriander leaves

finely grated rind of 1 lime

1 teaspoon vegetable oil

1 tablespoon mirin

2 teaspoons fish sauce

4 chunky salmon fillets, about 125 g (4 oz) each

400 g (13 oz) mixed stir-fry vegetables

- Put the ginger, chilli, coriander, lime rind, vegetable oil, mirin and fish sauce into a mini chopper or small food processor bowl and blend to a paste.

- Place the salmon fillets in a shallow dish and rub all over with the paste. Set aside to marinate for 10 minutes.

- Preheat the oven to 200°C (400°F), Gas Mark 6, and tear off four large sheets of foil and line with baking parchment. Put one-quarter of the stir-fry vegetables in the centre of each piece of baking parchment, then top each heap with a salmon fillet. Scrunch up the sides of the paper-lined foil to form an open parcel, then place on a baking sheet and bake in the oven for 10–12 minutes until the salmon is just cooked through.

- Remove from the oven and transfer the parcels to serving plates. Serve with steamed rice on the side, if liked.

 Thai Green Curry Salmon Stir-Fry Cut 625 g (1¼ lb) chunky salmon fillets into bite-sized pieces. Heat 1 teaspoon vegetable oil in a large frying pan over a medium heat, then add 2 tablespoons reduced-fat coconut milk from a 400 g (13 oz) can and 2–3 tablespoons green Thai curry paste. Stir-fry for 1 minute, then tip in the salmon and toss to coat. Add the remaining coconut milk, 2 teaspoons fish sauce and 1 teaspoon palm sugar. Simmer gently for 3–4 minutes until the salmon is cooked. Serve with steamed rice and garnish with coriander and lime wedges.

 Baked Salmon, Courgettes and Asparagus with Feta Slice 200 g (7 oz) baby courgettes in half lengthways and toss with 250 g (8 oz) trimmed asparagus and 1½ tablespoons olive oil. Season with salt and pepper, then place in a large roasting tin and put in a preheated oven, 200°C (400°F), Gas Mark 6, for 6–7 minutes. Meanwhile, take 4 chunky salmon fillets, about 125 g (4 oz) each, wrap each in 1 slice of smoked salmon and season with pepper. Remove the vegetables from the oven and place the salmon on top.

Crumble over 100 g (3½ oz) reduced-fat feta, scatter over 2 tablespoons pine nuts and drizzle with 2 tablespoons lemon juice. Return to the oven and roast for 7–8 minutes until the salmon is just cooked. Serve with steamed Mediterranean couscous.

Skewered Teriyaki Cod with Steamed Ginger Rice

Serves 4

6 tablespoons teriyaki sauce

500 g (1 lb) firm cod fillet, cut into bite-sized pieces

350 g (11½ oz) Thai jasmine rice

1 teaspoon salt

2 tablespoons finely chopped fresh root ginger

8 spring onions, trimmed

soy sauce, to serve

- Rub the teriyaki sauce over the pieces of cod and set aside to marinate.

- Put the rice in a saucepan with 750 ml (1¼ pints) of cold water, the salt and the ginger. Place the pan over a medium-high heat, bring to the boil and then reduce the heat to low and cover with a tight-fitting or foil-lined lid. Simmer gently for 12–14 minutes or until the water has been absorbed. Alternatively, cook in a rice cooker according to the manufacturer's instructions.

- Meanwhile, heat a ridged griddle pan and griddle the whole spring onions for 3–4 minutes until tender and charred, turning occasionally.

- Thread the cod on to 4 metal skewers, then place on a foil-lined baking sheet, slide under a preheated grill and grill for 2–3 minutes each side until cooked through.

- Serve the teriyaki cod with the rice, accompanied by the griddled spring onions and drizzled with any pan juices and a dash of soy sauce.

 Tuna Noodle Salad with Teriyaki Dressing Drain 2 x 185 g (6½ oz) cans tuna chunks in brine or spring water and toss with a 300 g (10 oz) bag of cooked, fresh rice noodles, 200 g (7 oz) bean sprouts and 1 deseeded and thinly sliced red pepper. Divide among 4 serving plates. Mix 2 tablespoons teriyaki sauce with 1 tablespoon honey and 2 tablespoons each of light soy sauce and lime juice. Drizzle over the noodle salad and serve.

 Teriyaki Tuna Burgers To make a teriyaki glaze, in a small saucepan heat 4 tablespoons teriyaki sauce with 2 tablespoons honey, 2 tablespoons light soy sauce, 1 finely chopped garlic clove, 1 teaspoon peeled and finely grated fresh root ginger and 1 teaspoon Japanese wasabi paste. When just starting to boil, reduce the heat and simmer to reduce the liquid by half. Meanwhile, finely chop 450 g (14½ oz) raw tuna and mix with 1 finely chopped shallot, 1 teaspoon Japanese wasabi paste and season with black pepper. Shape the tuna into 4 large burgers. Heat 1 tablespoon vegetable oil in a large, frying pan over medium heat and cook the burgers for 7–8 minutes until cooked through but still moist, turning and basting regularly with the teriyaki glaze. Meanwhile, griddle 8 trimmed spring onions as above. Serve the burgers in toasted, ciabatta-style rolls with 4 teaspoons mango chutney and the charred spring onions.

30 North African Tuna Fattoush Salad

Serves 4

2 large eggs
2 large pitta breads
2 tablespoons olive oil
4 tuna steaks, about 100 g (3½ oz) each
4 Little Gem lettuces, sliced
2 spring onions, sliced
1 small cucumber, deseeded and chopped
3 tomatoes, quartered, deseeded and chopped
1 green pepper, cored, deseeded and chopped
3 tablespoons flat leaf parsley, finely chopped
3 tablespoons mint, finely chopped
1–2 teaspoons harissa, to taste
2 tablespoons lemon juice
2 teaspoons crushed sumac, to sprinkle
salt and pepper

- Bring a small saucepan of water to the boil and add the eggs, taking care not to break the shells. Simmer gently for 6 minutes. Remove and cool under cold running water.

- Meanwhile, heat a ridged griddle pan and toast the pitta breads for 2–3 minutes, turning once, until toasted and nicely charred.

- Rub 1 tablespoon of the olive oil over the tuna steaks, then season with salt and pepper. Place on a baking sheet and slide under a preheated grill for 3–4 minutes until almost cooked, turning once. Set aside to cool.

- Cut up the toasted pitta bread and place in a large bowl with all the chopped vegetables and herbs. Mix together the harissa, lemon juice and remaining olive oil and stir into the salad, to coat. Season generously with salt and pepper.

- Divide the salad on to serving plates. Cut the eggs into wedges and arrange over the salads. Top each salad with a tuna steak and serve sprinkled with the crushed sumac.

 Tuna Salad and Harissa Pittas
Warm 4 wholemeal pitta breads and split open. Spread the inside of each pitta with ¼ teaspoon harissa and fill each one with 50 g (2 oz) drained tuna in spring water, ½ sliced Little Gem lettuce, ¼ thinly sliced spring onion, 4 thin slices of cucumber, 2 slices tomato and 1 teaspoon each of chopped parsley and mint. Squeeze over 1 teaspoon lemon juice and season well with salt and pepper.

 Grilled Tuna with Harissa-Spiced Pepper Sauce Heat 1 tablespoon olive oil in a large, nonstick frying pan over a medium heat and fry 2 sliced spring onions and 1 deseeded and chopped green pepper for 5–6 minutes until softened. Meanwhile, grill 4 tuna steaks, about 100 g (3½ oz) each, as above. Add 4 roughly chopped tomatoes, 3 tablespoons chopped flat leaf parsley, 3 tablespoons finely chopped mint, 1–2 teaspoons harissa, to taste, and 2 tablespoons lemon juice to the pan with the peppers and stir to heat. Season generously with salt and pepper and spoon into serving bowls. Top each dish with a tuna steak and serve immediately with warmed pitta breads.

 # Black Bean Chilli with Monkfish on Toasted Tortilla

Serves 4

2 tablespoons groundnut oil
1 teaspoon ground cumin
1 teaspoon ground coriander
¼ teaspoon ground cinnamon
¼ teaspoon chilli flakes
400 g (13 oz) monkfish tail, cubed
1 onion, finely chopped
2 garlic cloves, finely diced
200 ml (7 fl oz) red wine
500 ml (17 fl oz) passata
400 g (13 oz) can black beans, drained
few dashes of Tabasco sauce
4 large soft tortillas

Avocado salsa

1 large firm, ripe avocado
1½ tablespoons lime juice
½ small red onion, finely chopped
2 tomatoes, deseeded and diced
1 small bunch of coriander
salt and pepper

- Heat the oil in a heavy-based casserole over a medium heat, then add the spices and monkfish and cook for 2 minutes until lightly golden, stirring frequently. Remove the fish from the pan with a slotted spoon and set aside.

- Add the onion and garlic to the pan and cook for 5 minutes until softened, stirring frequently, then pour in the red wine and passata and add the black beans and a few shakes of Tabasco, to taste. Season with salt and pepper and simmer for 12–15 minutes until thickened.

- To make the avocado salsa, stone, peel and dice the avocado and gently mix in a small bowl with the lime juice. Add the onion and tomatoes. Finely chop the coriander and stir in, season with salt and pepper and mix well. Set aside.

- Stir the monkfish into the pan with the black bean chilli and simmer for a further 2–3 minutes until the fish is just cooked.

- Meanwhile, heat a ridged griddle pan over a medium-hot heat, toast the tortillas and place one on each plate. Spoon over the black bean chilli and monkfish and serve immediately with the avocado salsa.

 Black Bean and Monkfish Wrap

Toss 400 g (13 oz) cubed monkfish tail with 1 teaspoon each of ground cumin and ground coriander, ¼ teaspoon each of ground cinnamon and chilli flakes and 2 finely chopped garlic cloves. Heat 1 tablespoon groundnut oil in a nonstick pan over a medium heat, add the coated monkfish and fry, turning occasionally, for 5–6 minutes until just cooked through. Meanwhile, spread

150 g (5 oz) reduced-fat guacamole over 4 soft tortillas and scatter over a 400 g (13 oz) can of black beans, drained, ½ chopped small red onion, 1 chopped large bunch of coriander and 2 deseeded and diced tomatoes. Divide the spiced monkfish on to the tortillas and roll up tightly. Cut in half to serve.

Monkfish and Black Bean Stir-Fry

Heat 1 tablespoon vegetable oil in a frying pan, add 1 sliced onion, 2 sliced red peppers and cook for 3 minutes, stirring. Add 2 finely chopped garlic cloves, 1 tablespoon finely chopped fresh root ginger and stir. Add 400 g (13 oz) cubed monkfish tail and cook for 3 minutes. Stir in a 400 g (13 oz) can of black beans, drained, 200 g (7 oz) black bean stir-fry sauce and 2 tablespoons soy sauce. Simmer for 2 minutes and serve with rice.

Grilled Scallops with Chermoula Dressing

Serves 4

20 king scallops, without roes
350 g (11½ oz) green beans, trimmed
150 g (5 oz) watercress and spinach salad leaves

Chermoula dressing

1 small bunch of flat leaf parsley, roughly chopped
1 small bunch of coriander, roughly chopped
½ teaspoon ground cumin
½ teaspoon ground coriander
½ teaspoon turmeric
½ teaspoon ras el hanout
1 garlic clove, finely chopped
4 tablespoons lemon juice
1 tablespoon olive oil
salt and pepper

- To make the chermoula dressing, put the herbs, spices, garlic, lemon juice and oil in a mini chopper or a small food processor bowl and blend until smooth. Season with salt and pepper.

- Place the scallops in a large bowl and pour over half of the chermoula dressing. Mix well to coat, then set aside to marinate for 8–10 minutes.

- Meanwhile, place the green beans in a basket steamer and lower into a shallow pan of boiling water so that they are not quite touching the surface of the water. Steam for 3–4 minutes or until just tender. Alternatively, cook in an electric steamer. Toss the cooked beans in half of the remaining dressing and set aside.

- Arrange the scallops on a baking sheet and slide under a preheated grill for 3–4 minutes until just cooked through, turning occasionally.

- Toss the beans with the salad leaves and divide on to serving plates. Top the salad with the grilled scallops. Serve immediately with the remaining dressing on the side.

 Pan-Fried Scallops with Chermoula Salad Season 20 king scallops, without roes, with salt and pepper and heat 1 tablespoon olive oil in a large frying pan. Cook the scallops for 3–4 minutes until just cooked through, turning occasionally. Meanwhile, prepare the chermoula dressing as above. Halve 250 g (8 oz) mixed cherry tomatoes and toss with 150 g (5 oz) watercress. Divide between 4 serving plates. Arrange the scallops over the salads, drizzle with dressing and serve.

 Grilled Scallop with Spiced Chickpea and Bean Salad Cook 350 g (11½ oz) trimmed green beans as above. Heat 1 tablespoon olive oil in a frying pan over a medium heat, add 1 chopped onion and 2 chopped garlic cloves and cook for 6–7 minutes, stirring occasionally. Stir in the chermoula spices as above and fry for a further minute. Pour in 150 ml (¼ pint) dry white wine, 400 g (13 oz) can drained chickpeas and 250 g (8 oz) halved cherry tomatoes. Simmer for 5–6 minutes, then stir in 1 small bunch of roughly chopped parsley, 1 small bunch of roughly chopped coriander, the finely grated rind and juice of 1 lemon. Season with salt and pepper to taste, then stir in the green beans. Meanwhile, rub 2 teaspoons olive oil over 20 king scallops without roes, season with salt and pepper and slide under a preheated grill for 3–4 minutes until just cooked through. Serve with the spiced chickpeas and beans.

30 Steamed Sea Bass with Lemon Grass, Ginger and Noodles

Serves 4

2 spring onions, trimmed
4 sea bass fillets, about 125 g (4 oz) each
1 tablespoon groundnut oil
1 garlic clove, finely sliced
50 ml (2 fl oz) sake or Chinese cooking wine
350 g (11½ oz) buckwheat soba noodles
2 teaspoons sesame seeds, to garnish

Marinade

2 teaspoons caster sugar
2 tablespoons light soy sauce
2 lemon grass stalks, tough outer leaves removed, sliced
2 lime leaves, shredded
2.5 cm (1 inch) piece of fresh root ginger, cut into thin matchsticks

- Slice the spring onions very thinly lengthways and place in a bowl of cold water and ice cubes. Set aside in the fridge.

- To make the marinade, disolve the sugar in the soy sauce in a small bowl, then stir in the lemon grass, lime leaves and ginger.

- Score small, shallow slits into the skin side of the fillets and place them in flat dish. Pour the marinade over and rub it into the flesh. Set aside to marinade for 15 minutes.

- Meanwhile, heat the oil in a deep-sided frying pan over a medium heat. Fry the garlic for 2 minutes, then pour in the sake. Bubble to almost evaporate, then add the fish, skin side down, and any marinade. Cover with a lid and steam for 6–8 minutes until the fish is just cooked and the flesh flakes easily.

- Cook the soba noodles in a large pan of boiling water for 7–8 minutes, or according to the packet instructions, then drain.

- Remove the fillets from the pan, tip the noodles into the pan and toss to coat in the cooking juices. Pile the noodles on to serving plates and place the sea bass on top. Drain the spring onions and sprinkle over each fillet with the sesame seeds.

 Sea Bass and Roast Vegetable Couscous
Heat 1 tablespoon olive oil in a large frying pan over a medium heat and fry 4 sea bass fillets, skin side down, for 3 minutes until golden. Reduce the heat, cover and steam for 3–4 minutes until cooked. Divide 500 g (1 lb) ready-made roasted vegetable couscous and 150 g (5 oz) rocket between 4 plates. Mix 1 tablespoon vegetable oil with 1 teaspoon each of rice vinegar, finely chopped lemon grass and ginger. Drizzle over the salad and serve the fish on top.

 Roasted Whole Sea Bass with Noodles and Sake Dressing Score shallow slits into both sides of 4 small whole, gutted and scaled sea bass. Mix 1 teaspoon finely grated fresh root ginger and 1 finely chopped garlic clove with 2 teaspoons sesame oil, then rub the mix all over the inside and the skin of the sea bass. Place the fish in a nonstick roasting tray, sprinkle with 2 teaspoons sesame seeds and place in a preheated oven, 200°C (400°F),

Gas Mark 6, for 10–12 minutes until the flesh flakes easily when pressed in the centre with a knife. Meanwhile, cook 350 g (11½ oz) buckwheat soba noodles according to the packet instructions, and place the marinade ingredients as above, and 50 ml (2 fl oz) sake in a small saucepan. Place over a medium-low heat and simmer for 4–5 minutes until fragrant. Serve the sea bass with the cooked noodles and drizzled with the hot aromatic sake.

# Salt and Pepper Tiger Prawns with Baby Corn and Mango Salsa

Serves 4

1 teaspoon coarse sea salt

1 teaspoon Chinese 5-spice powder

1 teaspoon cracked black pepper

½ teaspoon Szechuan peppercorns, crushed

pinch of cayenne pepper

500 g (1 lb) unshelled tiger prawns

8 reduced-fat soft flour tortillas

Baby corn and mango salsa

200 g (7 oz) baby corn, sliced into small rounds

2 spring onions, trimmed and finely chopped

1 red chilli, deseeded and finely chopped

1 small mango, diced

2 tablespoons ketjap manis or sweet soy sauce

- Mix together in a large bowl the sea salt, Chinese 5-spice powder and the black, Szechuan and cayenne peppers, then tip in the prawns and toss until well coated in the spices.

- Heat a ridged griddled pan over a high heat, arrange the prawns over the pan and cook for 4–5 minutes until the prawns have turned pink and are cooked but still juicy.

- Meanwhile, to make the baby corn and mango salsa, mix together the baby corn, spring onions, red chilli and diced mango and then stir in the ketjap manis or sweet soy sauce.

- Once the prawns are cooked, arrange them on serving plates with the tortillas and the mango salsa on the side (and a large bowl for the shells).

 Spicy Prawn and Sweetcorn Salad Toss 400 g (13 oz) of cooked, peeled prawns with a 200 g (7 oz) can of drained sweetcorn, 2 chopped spring onions, 1 chopped red chilli and 1 diced mango. Combine 2 tablespoons each of ketjap manis and vegetable oil, add black pepper, crushed Szechuan peppercorns and pinch of cayenne pepper as above. Spoon the salad over the tortillas and serve drizzled with the dressing.

 Peppered Prawn, Baby Corn and Mango Spring Rolls Mix 350 g (11½ oz) raw, peeled prawns with 1 teaspoon each of coarse sea salt, cracked black pepper and Chinese 5-spice powder, ½ teaspoon crushed Szechuan peppercorns and a pinch of cayenne pepper. Heat a ridged griddle pan over a medium-high and cook the prawns for 2–3 minutes as above. Remove from the heat and set aside to cool for

10–15 minutes. Meanwhile, make the baby corn and mango salsa, as above. Soak 12 large rice paper wrappers in water for 2–3 minutes or until soft, and thinly shred ½ an iceberg lettuce and 1 carrot. Take one wrapper and place a little lettuce and carrot in the centre, then top with a few of the prawns and a small spoonful of salsa. Fold in the sides and roll up firmly. Repeat with the remaining ingredients and serve immediately.

30 Stuffed Salmon with Ricotta and Spinach

Serves 4

500 g (1 lb) new potatoes
4 salmon fillets, about 150 g (5 oz) each
150 g (5 oz) wild rocket leaves
salt and pepper
lemon wedges, to serve

Ricotta and spinach filling

100 g (3½ oz) ricotta
1 teaspoon finely grated lemon rind
¼ teaspoon ground nutmeg
2 teaspoons wholegrain mustard
1 tablespoon chopped chives
100 g (3½ oz) frozen spinach, defrosted, drained of excess water and roughly chopped

- Put the potatoes into a large saucepan and cover with lightly salted water. Bring to the boil and cook for 18–20 minutes until tender.

- Meanwhile, preheat the oven to 200°C (400°F), Gas Mark 6 and make the ricotta and spinach filling. Mix together the ricotta, lemon rind, nutmeg, wholegrain mustard, chives and spinach and season generously with salt and pepper.

- Place the salmon fillets on a nonstick baking tray and score a slit horizontally along the centre of each fillet. Open out the slits and stuff each with the ricotta mixture. The mixture should fill the gap and create a little pile on top of each fillet.

- Bake the fillets in the oven for about 15 minutes, or until the flesh flakes easily when pressed in the centre with a knife.

- Drain the new potatoes, then return them to the pan, crush with a fork and season generously with salt and pepper. Serve the baked salmon with the crushed new potatoes, rocket leaves and lemon wedges.

 Gravalax, Cream Cheese and Spinach Open Sandwiches Mix together 150 g (5 oz) reduced-fat cream cheese, 1 teaspoon finely grated lemon rind, ¼ teaspoon ground nutmeg, 2 teaspoons wholegrain mustard, 1 tablespoon chopped chives and 100 g (3½ oz) frozen spinach, defrosted, drained and roughly chopped. Season well with salt and pepper, then spread over 8 slices of rye bread. Top each with a thin slice of gravalax, season with black pepper and serve with lemon wedges.

 Smoked Salmon, Spinach and Tomato Pasta Bring a saucepan of lightly salted water to the boil and cook 400 g (13 oz) farfalle pasta for 11 minutes until 'al dente', or according to the packet instructions. Drain and cool under running cold water. Meanwhile, place 125 g (4 oz) baby leaf spinach in a large bowl with the finely grated rind and juice of 1 lemon, 75 g (3 oz) ready-to-eat, slow-roasted tomatoes (not in oil) and 200 g (7 oz) smoked salmon, cut into strips. Tip in the cooked pasta and toss well. Divide the salmon pasta into serving bowls, drizzle over 1 tablespoon olive oil and scatter over 1 tablespoon chopped chives and 2 tablespoons toasted mixed seeds. Serve immediately.

 # Smoked Mackerel Pasta Salad

Serves 4

300 g (10 oz) conchiglie pasta
200 g (7 oz) green beans, trimmed
4 hot-smoked peppered boneless mackerel fillets
125 g (4 oz) mixed peppery salad
½ cucumber, cut in half lengthways, deseeded and cut into chunky pieces
2 spring onions, finely sliced
2 hard-boiled eggs, quartered

Dressing

100 ml (3½ fl oz) half-fat soured cream
1 tablespoon wholegrain mustard
1 teaspoon French mustard
2 tablespoons lemon juice
1 teaspoon chopped dill
1 teaspoon chopped tarragon
salt and pepper

- Bring a large saucepan of lightly salted water to the boil and cook the pasta for 11 minutes until 'al dente', or according to the packet instructions. Drain and cool under running cold water. Tip into a large bowl and set aside.

- Meanwhile, bring a medium-sized saucepan of lightly salted water to the boil and cook the beans in for 4–5 minutes until just tender. Drain into a colander, cool under running cold water and set aside.

- To make the dressing, mix together in a small bowl all the ingredients and season with salt and pepper.

- Flake the smoked mackerel fillets into large pieces into the bowl with the cooled pasta, then add the salad leaves, cucumber, spring onions and cooked beans. Dress with some of the dressing. Divide the pasta salad among serving bowls and top with the hard-boiled eggs. Serve with the dressing on the side.

 Quick Smoked Mackerel Pâté

Put 4 hot-smoked peppered boneless mackerel fillets in a small food processor bowl or blender with 150 g (5 oz) reduced-fat cream cheese with chives, 1 tablespoon creamed horseradish, 2 teaspoons lemon juice and 1 teaspoon each of chopped dill and tarragon and blend to a rough paste. Season with salt and pepper. Serve with a selection of raw vegetable crudités or slices of hot toast.

 Pan-Fried Mackerel with Grilled Polenta Cut 500 g (1 lb) ready-made polenta into 1.5 cm (¾ inch) slices and place under a preheated grill for 5–6 minutes, turning once. Coat 4 fresh mackerel fillets, about 150 g (5 oz) each, in 4 tablespoons flour and season with salt and pepper. Shake the fillets to remove any excess flour. Heat 1 tablespoon olive oil in a large, nonstick frying pan over a medium heat,

then place the fillets skin side down in the pan and cook, turning once, for 4–5 minutes until the flesh is opaque. Meanwhile, deseed ½ a cucumber and use a mandolin or vegetable peeler to thinly slice into long ribbons. Arrange the cucumber on serving plates with 125 g (4 oz) peppery mixed salad leaves and the polenta. Top with the crispy mackerel fillets and serve immediately with lemon wedges on the side.

30 Baked Haddock with Garlic Crumb Crust

Serves 4

1.25 kg (2½ lb) floury potatoes, such as King Edwards, chopped
15 g (½ oz) butter
2 leeks, trimmed and sliced
4 chunky, boneless haddock loins, about 150 g (5 oz) each
light olive oil spray
2 tablespoons chopped chives
3 tablespoons half-fat crème fraîche
400 g (13 oz) asparagus, steamed, to serve
lemon wedges, to serve
salt and pepper

Breadcrumb topping

100 g (3½ oz) fresh breadcrumbs
1 garlic clove, finely chopped
1 spring onion, finely chopped
50 g (2 oz) pitted black olives, finely chopped

- Preheat the oven to 200°C (400°F), Gas Mark 6. Boil the potatoes in a pan of salted water for 15 minutes until tender.

- Melt the butter in a small pan, add the leeks and cover. Cook for 10–12 minutes, stirring, until softened and lightly golden. Place the haddock on a lightly greased baking sheet.

- Meanwhile, make the breadcrumb topping by mixing the breadcrumbs with the garlic, spring onions and olives and 2–3 tablespoons water. Bring the mixture together and place clumps, slightly flattened, on top of the fish.

- Spray the fish lightly with oil spray and bake in the oven for 15–18 minutes until the breadcrumbs are crisp and the flesh flakes easily when pressed in the centre with a knife.

- Drain the potatoes and mash until smooth. Fold in the leeks, chives and crème fraîche and season generously with salt and pepper. Spoon the mash on to warmed serving plates and top with the haddock. Serve immediately with steamed asparagus and lemon wedges.

---

10 Grilled Haddock with Toasted Breadcrumbs and Mashed Potato Place 4 thin haddock fillets, about 125 g (4 oz) each, on a foil-lined baking sheet, drizzle with 2 teaspoons olive oil, season with salt and pepper and slide under a preheated grill for 5–7 minutes, depending on the thickness of the fish, until the flesh is white and flakes easily when pressed in the centre with a knife. Meanwhile, make the breadcrumb topping as above, replacing the water with

1 tablespoon light olive oil. Tip the topping into a large, nonstick frying pan over a medium heat and toast, stirring frequently, until crisp and golden. Heat 625 g (1¼ lb) ready-made mashed potato and spoon the potato on to serving plates. Place the haddock on top of the potato and sprinkle over the toasted breadcrumbs. Serve with lemon wedges on the side.

20 Smoked Haddock Potato Bake Warm 500 g (1 lb) ready-made, reduced-fat cheese sauce in a large pan. Stir in 350 g (11½ oz) skinless, cubed smoked haddock, 200 g (7 oz) frozen peas, 150 g (5 oz) can sweetcorn, drained, and 2 tablespoons chopped chives. Simmer for 3 minutes, then pour into an ovenproof dish. Cover with 625 g (1¼ lb) ready-made mashed potato and sprinkle with 75 g (3 oz) fresh breadcrumbs. Bake in a preheated oven, 200°C (400°F), Gas Mark 6, for 10–12 minutes until crisp.

30 'Roast' Spiced Tuna Loin with New Potatoes and Asparagus

Serves 4

500 g (1 lb) new potatoes
750 g (1½ lb) tuna loin
1½ tablespoons olive oil
350 g (11½ oz) trimmed
  asparagus tips
lemon wedges, to serve
  (optional)

Spice mix

2 teaspoons cumin seeds
2 teaspoons caraway seeds
2 teaspoons fennel seeds
1 teaspoon pink peppercorns

- Preheat the oven to 200°C (400°F), Gas Mark 6. Put the potatoes into a large saucepan and cover with lightly salted water. Bring to the boil and cook for 15–18 minutes until tender. Drain and keep warm.

- Meanwhile, make the spice mix. Place all the spices in a spice grinder or mini chopper and grind to a coarse powder. Sprinkle the spices over a chopping board.

- Rub the tuna loin with ½ tablespoon of the olive oil, then roll in the spice mix to coat. Heat the remaining oil in a frying pan over a medium heat, then sear the tuna for 8–10 minutes, turning frequently, until browned all over. Place the tuna in a small, nonstick roasting tin and bake in the oven for 10–12 minutes until cooked on the outside. Remove from the oven, cover with foil and set aside to rest for 4–5 minutes.

- Heat a ridged griddle pan over a high heat and cook the asparagus, turning occasionally, for 3–4 minutes until just tender and nicely charred. Once cooked, arrange on serving plates with the potatoes. Cut the tuna into slices and serve with the asparagus and lemon wedges, if liked.

 Griddled Asparagus Tuna Niçoise

Cook 350 g (11½ oz) trimmed asparagus tips in a basket steamer for 3–4 minutes until tender, then cool under cold running water. Pat dry with kitchen paper and arrange on serving plates with 175 g (6 oz) rocket leaves, 250 g (8 oz) canned tuna fillets in spring water, drained, ½ thinly sliced red onion and 2 sliced, hard-boiled eggs. Drizzle with 4 tablespoons reduced-fat herby dressing and serve immediately.

 Spiced Griddled Tuna Loin with Potatoes and Asparagus

Cook 500 g (1 lb) new potatoes in lightly salted boiling water and make the spice mix as above. Rub 1 tablespoon olive oil over 4 thick tuna steaks, about 150 g (5 oz) each, and coat in the ground spice mix. Heat a ridged griddle pan over a medium-high heat and griddle the tuna for 2–3 minutes each side, depending on the rareness desired. Remove from the heat and set aside to rest.

Meanwhile, steam 350 g (11½ oz) trimmed asparagus tips in a basket steamer in a shallow pan of boiling water for 3–4 minutes until tender; make sure the basket is not quite touching the surface of the water. Arrange the asparagus and potato on serving plates, then top with the tuna steaks. Serve with lemon wedges on the side.

10 Lemony Scallop Skewers with Rocket

Serves 4

400 g (13 oz) queen scallops, without roes
finely grated rind of 1 lemon, plus 1 tablespoon juice
3 teaspoons basil oil
50 g (2 oz) blanched hazelnuts
200 g (7 oz) wild rocket, washed
salt and pepper

- Preheat the grill. Place the scallops in a bowl with the lemon rind and 2 teaspoons of the basil oil and season with black pepper. Mix well to coat, then thread the scallops onto 4 metal skewers.

- Slide the skewers under the grill for 2–3 minutes until just cooked, turning occasionally. They are ready as soon as they are firm and opaque.

- Meanwhile, heat a small frying pan over a medium heat, then tip in the hazelnuts and dry-roast until golden, shaking the pan frequently. Tip the nuts into a small dish and crush lightly.

- Toss the rocket leaves with the remaining basil oil, the lemon juice and salt and pepper. Arrange on serving plates and top with the scallop skewers. Scatter over the hazelnuts and serve immediately.

 Scallops with Anchovies and Parma Ham Place 4 anchovy fillets in a mini chopper with 1 tablespoon capers, 1 teaspoon grated lemon rind, 2 tablespoons lemon juice, 1 small bunch of basil leaves, 1 small garlic clove and 2 teaspoons basil oil. Blend until finely chopped, then season with salt and pepper. Heat 1 teaspoon basil oil in a nonstick pan, add 4 slices thinly shredded Parma ham. and fry until coloured. Add 400 g (13 oz) queen scallops, without roes, and plenty of black pepper. Fry for 2 minutes or until the scallops are just cooked. Serve with rocket leaves and the salsa verde.

 Grilled Scallops Wrapped In Parma Ham with Lemony Mash Cook 1 kg (2 lb) peeled potatoes in a large saucepan of lightly salted water for 18–20 minutes until tender. Drain and then mash with 2 tablespoons lemon juice and 2 teaspoons basil oil. Season with salt and pepper. Meanwhile, heat 1 tablespoon basil oil in a small frying pan, add 2 chopped shallots and cook until softened. Remove from the heat and mix with the finely grated rind of 1 lemon, some black pepper, 100 g (3½ oz) fresh breadcrumbs and 50 g (2 oz) crushed dry-roasted

blanched hazelnuts as above. Wrap 16 king scallops, without roes, in 16 lean strips of Parma ham and place in an ovenproof dish. Spoon the breadcrumb topping on to the scallops, then slide under a preheated grill for 7–8 minutes until the scallops are just cooked and the breadcrumbs are golden. Serve with lemony mashed potato and rocket leaves.

30 Salmon Wrapped in Ham with Pan-Roasted Potatoes and Beans

Serves 4

8 lean slices Black Forest ham
1 large bunch of basil, leaves stripped and shredded
4 chunky skinless salmon fillets, about 125 g (4 oz) each, checked for pin bones
500 g (1 lb) baby new potatoes
1 tablespoon olive oil
350 g (11½ oz) runner beans, trimmed
250 g (8 oz) green beans, trimmed
1 tablespoon lemon juice
salt and cracked black pepper
2 tablespoons balsamic glaze, to drizzle

- Lay the ham on a board to form 4 crosses. Scatter the centre of each cross with a pinch of the shredded basil and some cracked black pepper. Place the salmon, skin side up, on the basil and fold over the ham to completely enclose.

- Put the potatoes in a large saucepan with the olive oil and season with salt and pepper. Cover and fry gently over a medium-low heat, shaking the pan frequently, for 20 minutes.

- Meanwhile, bring a saucepan of lightly salted water to the boil and cook the two types of beans for 2–3 minutes until firm but tender. Drain and toss with the lemon juice, remaining basil leaves and some cracked black pepper.

- Heat a ridged griddle pan and cook the wrapped salmon fillets for 6–7 minutes, turning once, until the ham is golden and crispy and the salmon is almost cooked through. Remove from the heat and set aside the salmon to rest.

- Toss the cooked potatoes quickly with the dressed beans and spoon immediately onto warmed plates. Serve with the salmon parcels and drizzle with the balsamic glaze.

 Smoked Salmon, Black Forest Ham and Basil Tagliatelle Cook 500 g (1 lb) fresh tagliatelle in a large saucepan of salted boiling water, according to the packet instructions. Drain and toss with 350 g (11½ oz) flaked hot smoked salmon, 2 tablespoons lemon juice, 1 large bunch of basil, leaves stripped and shredded, 4 lean slices Black Forest ham, roughly chopped. Season with plenty of black pepper and serve with 175 g (6 oz) peppery mixed salad leaves.

 Crispy Salmon Fillets with New Potatoes and Green Beans Chop 500 g (1 lb) baby new potatoes in half and cook in a saucepan of lightly salted boiling water for 12–15 minutes until tender. Heat 1 tablespoon olive oil in a large, nonstick frying pan over a medium heat and pan-fry 4 tail end salmon fillets, about 125 g (4 oz) each, skin side down, for 4–5 minutes until cooked but still moist. Once the skin is crisp, turn off the heat, scatter over the shredded basil leaves from 1 large bunch of basil, reserving a few whole leaves to garnish, and season with a little salt and pepper. Cover with a lid and set aside for 4–5 minutes to keep warm. Meanwhile, prepare and cook 350 g (11½ oz) runner beans and 250 g (8 oz) green beans as above. Transfer the potatoes and beans to serving plates and top with the salmon fillets. Garnish with the reserved whole basil leaves and serve with lemon wedges on the side.

LOW-FISH-BIZ

Pasta with Tuna and Aubergine Arrabiata

Serves 4

1 tablespoon olive oil
1 onion, finely chopped
2 garlic cloves, finely chopped
1 aubergine, diced
650 g (1 lb 7 oz) passata
100 ml (3½ fl oz) red wine
½–1 teaspoon chilli flakes, to taste
75 g (3 oz) pitted green olives
    with hot chilli peppers or
    chilli-stuffed olives, sliced
1 small bunch of basil, leaves
    stripped
pinch of sugar
400 g (13 oz) penne rigate
2 x 185 g (6½ oz) cans tuna
    chunks in spring water, drained
finely grated Parmesan cheese,
    to serve (optional)
salt and pepper

- Heat the oil in a large, deep-sided frying pan over a medium heat, add the onion and garlic and cook for 4–5 minutes, stirring occasionally, until softened and lightly golden.

- Bring two pans of lightly salted water to the boil. Add the aubergine to one saucepan and cook for 3–4 minutes until almost tender, then tip into a colander and drain well.

- Meanwhile, pour the passata and red wine into the pan with the onions, add the chilli flakes, olives, basil and sugar and season with salt and pepper. Add the well-drained aubergines and bring to the boil, then reduce the heat and simmer gently for 12–15 minutes until thickened slightly.

- While the sauce is simmering, cook the pasta in the second pan of boiling water for 11 minutes until 'al dente', or according to the packet instructions.

- Drain the pasta, stir the tuna into the sauce, add the pasta and serve with a little Parmesan sprinkled over, if liked.

Pasta with Aubergine and Tomato Sauce

Cook 500 g (1 lb) fresh penne in salted boiling water according to the packet instructions. Meanwhile, roughly chop 6 ripe tomatoes and 200 g (7 oz) grilled aubergines or mixed antipasti and fry over a medium heat. Add 75 g (3 oz) sliced chilli-stuffed olives, chopped leaves from 1 small bunch of basil, 1 deseeded and finely chopped red chilli and stir. Drain the pasta, add the tomato mixture to the pasta and stir to combine. Serve.

Aubergine and Tomato Pasta Bake

Fry 1 finely chopped onion and 2 finely chopped garlic cloves in 1 tablespoon olive oil over a medium heat until softened and lightly golden. Add 100 ml (3½ fl oz) red wine, ½–1 teaspoon chilli flakes, to taste, 75 g (3 oz) sliced pitted green olives with hot chilli peppers or chilli-stuffed olives, 200 g (7 oz) well-drained, grilled aubergines or mixed antipasti, 2 x 400 g (13 oz) can cherry tomatoes and a pinch of sugar. Season well with salt and pepper, then simmer for

7–8 minutes until thickened slightly. Meanwhile, cook 500 g (1 lb) fresh penne in lightly salted boiling water for 5–6 minutes until 'al dente', or according to the packet instructions. Drain the pasta and mix with the tomato sauce until well combined, then tip into an ovenproof dish, sprinkle with 2 tablespoons grated Parmesan cheese and place in a preheated oven, 220 °C (425 °F), Gas Mark 7, for 12–15 minutes until bubbling and crispy. Serve with a crisp green salad.

QuickCook
Meat and Poultry

Recipes listed by cooking time

30

Grilled Tandoori Chicken Skewers with Cucumber and Cumin Salad 140

Asian-Spiced Beef Carpaccio 142

Piri-Piri Spiced Turkey Fillets and Hummus 144

Beef and Baby Beetroot Salad with Horseradish Dressing 146

Chicken Filo Pastries with Plum Sauce 148

Pork and Rosemary Meatballs with Mixed Bean Salad 150

Grilled Mini-Turkey Ball Skewers with Spicy Salsa 152

Chilli Con Carne 154

Roasted Sweet Chilli Chicken with Vegetable Stir-Fry 156

'Meat Feast' Italian Pizza 158

Baked Chicken Parcels with Mozzarella and Basil 160

Sweet and Spicy Pork with Red Peppers 162

Baked Jerk and Mustard Chicken and Coleslaw 164

Chinese 5-Spice Duck with Ramen Noodles 166

Mild and Creamy Chicken Curry 168

Lebanese Lamb Skewers with Cucumber Salad 170

Chinese-Style Traybake 172

Gnocchi, Squash, Sweet Potato and Blue Cheese Bake 174

Pan-Fried Steak with New Potatoes and Rocket Salad 176

Crispy Garlic Baked Stuffed Chicken Breasts 178

Moroccan Lamb Skewers with Preserved Lemon Couscous 180

Penne Bolognaise Bake 182

Roast Pork Tenderloin with Lemon, Sage and Capers 184

Warmed Roasted Tomato and Serrano Ham Pasta 186

Stuffed Pork Steaks with Butter Bean Salad 188

Chicken Risotto with White Wine and Asparagus 190

Poached Poussin with Baby Vegetables 192

Madeira and Rosemary Pork Medallions 194

Roasted Turkey, Prosciutto, Sage and Caperberry Rolls 196

Grilled Barbecue Pork Skewers with Crunchy Coleslaw 198

20

Grilled Tandoori Chicken 140

Stir-Fried Beef Pancake Rolls 142

Quick Piri-Piri Turkey Steaks with Hummus 144

Rare Beef and Blue Cheese Pasta 146

Steamed Chinese Chicken and Noodle Salad 148

Pork Skewers with Warm Bean Salad 150

Turkey Burgers with Spicy Salsa 152

Chilli and Lettuce Wraps 154

Sweet Chilli Chicken Stir-Fry 156

'Meat Feast' Thin and Crisp Tortilla-Based Pizza 158

Grilled Chilli Pesto Chicken with Warm Couscous Salad 160

Sweet and Sour Chicken 162

Honey and Mustard Glazed Chicken Fillets with Coleslaw 164

Duck and Egg Noodle Stir-Fry 166

Grilled Korma Chicken with Rice 168

10

30 Grilled Tandoori Chicken Skewers with Cucumber and Cumin Salad

Serves 4

175 g (6 oz) fat-free Greek yogurt, plus extra to serve
2 tablespoons tandoori paste
500 g (1 lb) skinless chicken breast fillets, cut into strips
2 teaspoons cumin seeds
1 small cucumber
½ red onion, cut in half and finely sliced
3 tablespoons fresh coriander leaves
2 lemons, cut into wedges
salt and pepper
reduced-fat mini naan breads, to serve (optional)

- Mix together the yogurt and tandoori paste in a large bowl, add the chicken and toss until the chicken is well coated. Set aside to marinate for 10 minutes.

- Heat a small frying pan over a medium heat, add the cumin seeds and dry-roast for 1–2 minutes, stirring frequently. Remove from the heat when the seeds become fragrant and begin to smoke.

- Thread the chicken strips on to 8 small metal skewers and lay on a foil-lined baking tray. Cook under a preheated grill for 8–10 minutes until the chicken is cooked through, turning once.

- Meanwhile, slice the cucumber into ribbons using a sharp vegetable peeler and arrange on 4 serving plates. Scatter the onion and coriander over the cucumber, sprinkle over the toasted cumin seeds and season lightly with salt and pepper. Place the chicken and lemon wedges on top and. serve immediately with warm naan breads and extra yogurt.

 Tandoori Chicken and Salad Naans

Stir together 1 teaspoon tandoori paste and 6 tablespoons fat-free natural yogurt in a bowl. Roughly slice 300 g (10 oz) cooked chicken fillets and mix with the tandoori yogurt. Cut ½ cucumber into ribbons, using a vegetable peeler, and finely slice ½ red onion. Divide the chicken into 4 low-fat mini nann breads, then divide the cucumber, onion, ½ teaspoon cumin seeds and a few coriander leaves into the naans. Squeeze a little lemon juice over the salad and serve immediately.

 Grilled Tandoori Chicken

Cut 500 g (1 lb) skinless chicken fillets into strips and mix with 2 tablespoons tandoori paste in a bowl until well coated. Place the chicken on a foil-lined baking sheet and slide under a preheated grill for 6–7 minutes until cooked through, turning occasionally. Meanwhile, make a simple raita by mixing together 175 g (6 oz) fat-free Greek yogurt, 2 teaspoons lemon juice, ¾ teaspoon ground cumin and salt and pepper, to taste. Serve the chicken with the raita and warmed naan breads.

30 Asian-Spiced Beef Carpaccio

Serves 4

1 tablespoon groundnut oil
625 g (1¼ lb) fillet steak
200 g (7 oz) bean sprouts
2 spring onions, finely sliced
small bunch of mint, finely chopped
small bunch of coriander, chopped
3 tablespoons chopped blanched
   peanuts (optional)

Dressing

1 tablespoon groundnut oil
1 teaspoon fish sauce
2 teaspoons rice vinegar
2 tablespoons light soy sauce
2 teaspoons palm sugar
1 lemon grass stalk, outer leaves
   discarded and finely chopped
1 banana shallot, finely chopped
1 red chilli, deseeded, finely sliced

- Heat the oil in a nonstick frying pan over a medium-hot heat, add the beef fillet and sear for 4–5 minutes, turning frequently, until browned all over but still rare. Remove the fillet from the pan, pat dry with kitchen paper and wrap in clingfilm. Place in the freezer to chill for 20 minutes.

- Meanwhile, mix together all the dressing ingredients in a small bowl until well combined.

- In another bowl toss together the bean sprouts, spring onion, mint and coriander leaves.

- Remove the beef from the freezer, discard the clingfilm and place on a chopping board. Slice the beef as thinly as possible, then arrange on 4 large plates, overlapping the slices slightly.

- Scatter the bean sprout mix over the beef carpaccio, drizzle over the dressing, scatter with the peanuts and serve.

 Asian-Spiced Bean Sprout Salad with Roast Beef Mix together 1 tablespoon groundnut oil, 1 teaspoon fish sauce, 2 teaspoons each of rice vinegar and palm sugar, 2 tablespoons light soy sauce and 1 teaspoon each finely chopped lemon grass, finely grated fresh root ginger and finely chopped red chilli in a large bowl. Add 200 g (7 oz) bean sprouts and toss to coat. Serve with 400 g (13 oz) cooked and sliced rare beef, sprinkled with chopped coriander and mint and 3 tablespoons chopped peanuts.

 Stir-Fried Beef Pancake Rolls Heat 1 tablespoon groundnut oil in a wok over a medium-high heat, add 1 sliced onion and stir-fry for 2 minutes. Add 1 tablespoon finely chopped fresh root ginger and 1 deseeded and sliced medium red chilli and stir-fry for a further 30 seconds. Add 300 g (10 oz) thin beef strips and stir-fry for 2 minutes. Tip in 200 g (7 oz) thinly sliced, mixed stir-fry vegetables and 200 g (7 oz) bean sprouts and cook for a further 2–3 minutes, then pour in 250 g (8 oz) plum and hoisin stir-fry sauce and stir for 1 minute or until heated through. Serve with 12–16 Chinese pancakes, 2 trimmed and sliced spring onions and half a cucumber, cut into batons, to make pancake rolls at the table.

30 Piri-Piri Spiced Turkey Fillets and Hummus

Serves 4

450 g (14½ oz) turkey breast fillets, cut into strips
400 g (13 oz) can chickpeas, drained
1 tablespoon lime juice
5–6 tablespoons low-fat soured cream
4 multiseed tortillas, warmed
lime wedges
salt and pepper

Piri-piri marinade

2 tablespoons sun-dried tomato paste
1 teaspoon oregano
2 tablespoons red wine vinegar
1 teaspoon hot smoked paprika
2 garlic cloves, finely chopped
2 long red chillies, finely chopped (deseed for less heat)

- To make the piri-piri marinade, put the tomato paste, oregano, red wine vinegar, paprika, garlic and chillies in a mini chopper or the small bowl of a food processor. Season generously with salt and pepper, then blend until smooth.

- Tip the turkey strips into a bowl and scrape over the piri-piri marinade, reserving 1 tablespoon to make the hummus. Mix all the ingredients until the turkey is well coated in the marinade, then set aside to marinate.

- Meanwhile, place the chickpeas, lime juice and reserved piri-piri marinade in a food processor or blender and pulse briefly, adding enough soured cream to give a smooth, creamy consistency.

- Arrange the marinated turkey strips on a foil-lined baking tray and slide under a preheated grill for 5–7 minutes, turning frequently, until cooked and lightly charred.

- Serve the grilled turkey fillets with the hummus, warmed tortillas and lime wedges on the side.

 Griddled Tortilla with Piri-Piri Chicken Salad Heat a ridged griddle pan over a medium-high heat and griddle the tortillas for 30–60 seconds each side, or until charred but still slightly soft. Push the tortillas into 4 small, deep serving bowls so that they line the bowls. Meanwhile, mix together 1 tablespoon ready-made piri-piri sauce and 6 tablespoons extra-light mayonnaise in a large bowl. Add 300 g (10 oz) cooked, shredded turkey breast, then fold until the turkey is well coated in the mayonnaise. Fill the tortilla-lined bowls with 1 shredded iceberg lettuce, then spoon the turkey mixture over the top. Sprinkle each salad with a pinch of hot smoked paprika and serve immediately with lime wedges on the side.

 Quick Piri-Piri Turkey Steaks with Hummus Place 4 turkey breast steaks between 2 sheets of clingfilm and batter with a rolling pin to flatten. Coat the turkey steaks with 4 tablespoons ready-made piri-piri sauce, then place on a foil-lined grill tray and slide under a preheated grill for 5–7 minutes until cooked, turning once. Stir 2 teaspoons of the ready-made piri-piri sauce into 300 g (10 oz) reduced-fat hummus. Serve the turkey steaks with the hummus, warm tortillas and lime wedges.

30 Rare Beef and Baby Beetroot Salad with Horseradish Dressing

Serves 4

250 g (8 oz) small, unpeeled baby beetroot, green stalks removed

2 lean rump or sirloin steaks, about 200 g (7 oz) each, trimmed

2 teaspoons olive oil

finely grated rind of 1 lemon, and 1½ tablespoons lemon juice

1 garlic clove, finely chopped

2 tablespoons finely chopped chives

175 g (6 oz) runner beans, sliced

1 teaspoon horseradish sauce

1 teaspoon clear honey

3 tablespoons reduced-fat soured cream

10 radishes, thinly sliced

50 g (2 oz) walnut pieces

125 g (4 oz) bistro-style salad leaves

salt and pepper

- Cook the beetroot in a saucepan of boiling water for 10–25 minutes, depending on the size of the beetroots, until tender.

- Meanwhile, place the steaks in a shallow dish with the olive oil, lemon rind, garlic, 1 tablespoon of the chopped chives and plenty of cracked black pepper. Toss until the steaks are well coated in the marinade.

- Bring another saucepan of water to the boil and cook the runner beans for 1–2 minutes until almost tender. Drain and cool immediately under cold running water.

- Heat a ridged griddle pan over a medium-high heat and griddle the steaks for 1 minute each side until charred but still pink. Set aside in a warm place to rest.

- Mix the lemon juice, horseradish, honey, soured cream and remaining chives in a bowl and season with salt and pepper. Drain the beetroot, cut into wedges and toss with the cooked beans, radishes, walnuts and salad leaves, then heap on to serving plates. Slice the beef thinly and arrange over each salad, drizzle over the horseradish dressing and serve.

1 **Bistro-Style Salad with Rare Beef and Blue Cheese Dressing** Make the baby beetroot salad as above. Make a blue cheese dressing by combining 1½ tablespoons lemon juice, 1 teaspoon clear honey, 1 tablespoon snipped chives, 3 tablespoons reduced-fat soured cream and 50 g (2 oz) strong blue cheese, such as Gorgonzola Piccante. Serve with 400 g (13 oz) hand-carved, rare-cooked beef on top. Drizzle over the blue cheese dressing and serve.

2 **Rare Beef and Blue Cheese Pasta** Cook 400 g (13 oz) farfalle pasta in lightly salted boiling water for 11 minutes until 'al dente', or according to the packet instructions. Meanwhile, griddle 2 trimmed lean rump or sirloin steaks, about 200 g (7 oz) each, as above, and thinly slice. Make a blue cheese dressing by mixing together 1½ tablespoons lemon juice, 1 teaspoon honey, 1 tablespoon snipped chives, 3 tablespoons reduced-fat

soured cream and 50 g (2 oz) strong blue cheese, such as Gorgonzola Piccante or Stilton, until well combined. Cook the runner beans in a saucepan of boiling water for 1–2 minutes until almost tender. Drain the pasta and mix with the blue cheese dressing, 50 g (2 oz) walnuts pieces, the runner beans and the beef. Serve immediately, garnished with snipped chives and with a bistro-style salad as a side dish.

LOW-MEAT-GAL

Chinese Chicken Wraps with Plum Sauce

Serves 4

4 large reduced-fat tortilla bread wraps

4 tablespoons plum sauce, plus extra to serve (optional)

300 g (10 oz) cooked chicken breasts, such as sweet chilli cooked chicken, sliced

½ cucumber, cut into batons

3 spring onions, trimmed and finely sliced lengthways

1 large romaine lettuce heart, shredded

- Spread the tortilla bread wraps with the plum sauce, then top each wrap with the chicken, cucumber and spring onions. Finish with the romaine lettuce and roll up tightly.

- Cut in half diagonally and serve with a little extra plum sauce, if liked.

 Steamed Chinese Chicken and Noodle Salad Put 400 g (13 oz) raw chicken strips, 1 teaspoon finely grated fresh root ginger and 2 tablespoons dark soy sauce in a bowl and mix until the chicken is well coated. Place the chicken in a large basket steamer and lower into a shallow saucepan of boiling water so that the basket does not quite touching the surface of the water. Steam for 5–7 minutes until the chicken is cooked through. Set aside to cool. Meanwhile, cook 500 g (1 lb) fresh noodles in boiling water for 2–3 minutes until tender, then drain into a colander and cool under running cold water. Toss together 1 shredded carrot, 1 thinly sliced red pepper, 200 g

(7 oz) beansprouts and the noodles in a large bowl. In a separate bowl mix together 4 tablespoons plum sauce, 1 teaspoon finely grated fresh root ginger, 1 teaspoon sesame oil and 2 tablespoons light soy sauce. Scatter the steamed chicken over the noodles and drizzle with the dressing. Serve immediately.

Chicken Filo Pastries with Plum Sauce Mix together in a bowl 400 g (13 oz) cooked, shredded chicken, 3 finely sliced spring onions, 1 grated carrot, 100 g (3½ oz) finely shredded mangetout and 1 finely chopped small bunch of coriander until combined. Cut 8 sheets of filo pastry to 15 x 25 cm (6 x 10 inches). Put one-eighth of the chicken mixture along the end of one rectangle, leaving a gap at the edge. Fold in the longer pastry sides, then roll up into a cigar shape. Brush with melted butter to seal and repeat to make 8 pastries. Place on a lightly greased baking sheet and cook in a preheated oven, 200°C (400°F), Gas Mark 6, for 18–20 minutes until golden and crisp. Serve with plum sauce.

LOW-MEAT-DOU

30 Pork and Rosemary Meatballs with Mixed Bean Salad

Serves 4

750 g (1½ lb) lean minced pork
75 g (3 oz) fresh breadcrumbs
1 egg, lightly beaten
1 tablespoon chopped rosemary
1 teaspoon fennel seeds, toasted
finely grated rind of 1 lemon
1 garlic clove, finely chopped
2 tablespoons olive oil
100 ml (3½ fl oz) dry white wine
500 g (1 lb) passata
salt and pepper

Warm bean salad

100 ml (3½ fl oz) dry white wine
2 x 400 g (13 oz) can butter beans
400 g (13 oz) can borlotti beans
12 slow roasted tomatoes (not in
   oil), chopped
1 teaspoon fennel seeds, toasted
juice of 1 lemon

- Place the minced pork, breadcrumbs, egg, rosemary, fennel seeds, lemon rind and garlic in a large bowl. Season with salt and pepper, then mix well to thoroughly combine. Shape into about 24 small meatballs.

- Heat the oil in a large, nonstick frying pan over a medium heat, then fry the meatballs, turning frequently, for 10–12 minutes until cooked through and browned all over.

- Pour 100 ml of the white wine into the pan with the meatballs and bubble to evaporate. Add the passata and simmer for 10 minutes, occasionally scraping the sticky bits away from the bottom of the pan.

- Meanwhile, to make the warm bean salad, pour the white wine into a large saucepan and bring to the boil. Drain the beans and add with the slow-roasted tomatoes and fennel seeds. Season with salt and pepper. Simmer for 5 minutes, then stir in 4 tablespoons of the sauce from the meatballs, the lemon juice and the parsley. Spoon the bean mix into serving bowls, top with the meatballs and serve.

 Warm Bean and Crispy Bacon Salad

Place 8 slices of lean smoked back bacon under a preheated grill and cook for 3–4 minutes until crispy, turning once. Meanwhile, pour 100 ml (3½ fl oz) dry white wine into a large saucepan and bring to the boil. Add 2 drained 400 g (13 oz) cans butter beans, 1 drained 400 g (13 oz) can borlotti beans, 12 chopped ready-to-eat slow roasted tomatoes (not in oil) and 1 teaspoon toasted fennel seeds. Season with and salt and pepper and simmer for 5 minutes,

then add the juice of 1 lemon and 1 chopped large bunch of parsley. Divide the warmed bean salad onto serving plates, then cut the bacon into slices and sprinkle over the beans. Serve with slices of warmed, herby bread.

 Pork Skewers with Warm Bean Salad

Mix 1 tablespoon finely chopped rosemary, 2 teaspoons toasted fennel seeds, the grated rind of 1 lemon and 1 tablespoon olive oil in a bowl. Tip in 625 g (1¼ lb) lean pork loin, cubed, and toss until coated. Thread the pork on to 8 metal skewers and cook under a preheated grill for 8–10 minutes, turning frequently. Make the bean salad as above, substituting the passata with 2 tablespoons sun-dried tomato paste. Serve the pork with the warm salad.

LOW-MEAT-BED

 # Turkey Burgers with Spicy Salsa

Serves 4

500 g (1 lb) lean minced turkey
finely grated rind of 1 lime
3 spring onions, trimmed
1 tablespoon sweet soy sauce or
  ketjap manis
1 teaspoon ground cumin
100 g (3½ oz) fresh breadcrumbs
1 small egg, lightly beaten
4 small ciabatta-style buns
2 romaine lettuce hearts,
  shredded, to serve

Spicy Salsa

250 g (8 oz) cherry tomatoes,
  quartered
1 red chilli, deseeded and finely
  chopped
2 spring onions, finely sliced
1 tablespoon lime juice
1 tablespoon sweet soy sauce or
  ketjap manis
1 small bunch of coriander,
  chopped
1 firm, ripe avocado

- Place the minced turkey in a large bowl with the lime rind, spring onions, soy sauce, cumin, breadcrumbs and egg. Mix until well combined then form into 8 flattened patties.

- Transfer the burgers to a grill rack and slide under a preheated grill for 3–4 minutes each side until browned and cooked through.

- Meanwhile, make the spicy salsa by putting all the salsa ingredients in a bowl and stir until well combined. Set aside.

- Cut the ciabatta rolls in half and place the rolls, cut side up, on a grill rack. Slide under a preheated grill and toast for 1–2 minutes until lightly charred.

- When the burgers are ready, place them on the toasted rolls with the romaine lettuce leaves and top with the salsa. Serve as open burgers.

 Healthy Turkey and Salsa Granary Baguettes Make the spicy salsa as above. Cut 4 small granary baguettes in half lengthways and fill each baguette with one-quarter of a 75 g (3 oz) bag of mixed leaves, 1 thick slice of cooked, hand-carved roast turkey and 1–2 spoonfuls of the salsa, then serve.

 **Grilled Mini-Turkey Ball Skewers with Spicy Salsa** Place 500 g (1 lb) lean minced turkey, ½ finely chopped red onion, 1 finely chopped small bunch of parsley, 1 finely chopped red chilli and 1 teaspoon each of ground cumin, ground coriander and fennel seeds and mix until well combined. Season generously with salt and pepper, form into 32 small balls and thread onto 8 metal skewers. Place the skewers on a grill rack and slide under a preheated grill for 10–12 minutes until cooked through, turning occasionally. Meanwhile, make the spicy salsa as above. Serve the skewers with toasted ciabatta and the salsa.

30 Chilli Con Carne

Serves 4

1 tablespoon groundnut oil
1 large onion, chopped
500 g (1 lb) lean beef, such as rump or sirloin, cut into strips
2 garlic cloves, finely chopped
1 teaspoon ground cumin
1 teaspoon ground coriander
¼ teaspoon ground cinnamon
1–1½ teaspoons chilli flakes, to taste
250 ml (8 fl oz) Mexican lager
625 g (1¼ lb) thick passata
1 tablespoon Dijon mustard
400 g (13 oz) can kidney beans, drained
long-grain rice, to serve
small bunch of coriander, chopped, to garnish

- Heat the oil in a large, deep-sided frying pan or a casserole dish over a medium heat. Fry the onions for 5–6 minutes, stirring occasionally, until lightly coloured and just beginning to soften.

- Meanwhile, put the beef, garlic, ground spices and chilli flakes, to taste, in a bowl and toss until the beef is well coated. Scrape the beef into the pan with the onions, increase the heat to medium-high and stir-fry for 1–2 minutes or until the meat is browned.

- Add the lager, passata, mustard and kidney beans to the pan and bring to the boil. Reduce the heat, then leave to cook at a quick simmer for about 20 minutes or until thickened.

- Meanwhile, bring a large saucepan of lightly salted water to the boil and cook the rice for 15 minutes until tender, or according to the packet instructions.

- Serve the chilli with the rice or with baked potatoes, sprinkled with the coriander and a dash of Tabasco and with lime wedges on the side, if liked.

Quick Chilli Con Carne Burgers

Combine 2 tablespoons chilli con carne seasoning mix with 400 g (13 oz) lean minced beef in a bowl, then form into 4 flattened burgers. Place on a grill rack under a preheated grill for 2–3 minutes each side or until cooked through and serve with 4 wholemeal buns and a handful of salad leaves.

Chilli Con Carne and Lettuce Wraps

Cut 500 g (1 lb) lean beef, such as rump or sirloin, into strips. Put the beef in a bowl and mix with 2 finely chopped garlic cloves, 1 teaspoon each of ground cumin and coriander, ¼ teaspoon ground cinnamon and 1–1½ teaspoons chilli flakes, to taste, until combined. Heat 1 tablespoon groundnut oil in a large frying pan, add the onion and stir-fry for 4–5 minutes until softened. Add the beef and stir-fry for a further 4–5 minutes until cooked. Heap the beef and onion mix on to 4 reduced-fat tortilla wraps. Top each wrap with ¼ of the drained beans from a 400 g (13 oz) can, shredded iceberg lettuce, a dollop of reduced-fat soured cream and a few shakes of Tabasco sauce. Serve immediately.

20 Sweet Chilli Chicken Stir-Fry

Serves 4

1 tablespoon groundnut oil

500 g (1 lb) free-range chicken breast, cut into bite-sized pieces

1 large onion, cut into large pieces

2 garlic cloves, sliced

1 tablespoon finely chopped fresh root ginger

100 g (3½ oz) pineapple, peeled and 'eyes' remove, sliced and cut into wedges

250 g (8 oz) sweet chilli stir-fry sauce

150 g (5 oz) water chestnuts, halved

1 tablespoon soy sauce

1 tablespoon lime juice

125 g (4 oz) frozen peas

2 tablespoons roughly chopped unsalted cashew nuts

- Heat the oil in a wok or large frying pan over a medium heat. Tip in the chicken pieces and cook for 3–4 minutes, stirring frequently, until golden brown all over. Remove from the heat with a slotted spoon and set aside.

- Add the onion to the wok and stir-fry for 2–3 minutes until golden and beginning to soften, then add the garlic and ginger and stir-fry for 1–2 minutes. Stir in the pineapple and sweet chilli sauce, then bring to a boil.

- Return the chicken to the pan with the water chestnuts, soy sauce and lime juice and stir to combine. Reduce the heat and simmer gently for 4–6 minutes until the chicken is cooked through, then add the peas and stir for 1–2 minutes until hot. Scatter over the cashew nuts and serve immediately with steamed rice.

 Quick Sweet Chilli Chicken Stir-Fry

Heat 2 teaspoons groundnut oil in a large frying pan. Add 1 teaspoon each of finely chopped garlic and fresh root ginger. Stir-fry for 30 seconds. Add 400 g (13 oz) prepared stir-fry vegetables and fry for 3–4 minutes, then add 400 g (13 oz) cooked chicken slices, 100 g (3½ oz) pineapple cut into bite-sized wedges, 250 g (8 oz) sweet chilli stir-fry sauce, 1 tablespoon soy sauce and 1 tablespoon lime juice. Stir until hot, then spoon into deep bowls over 500 g (1 lb) hot, precooked rice.

 Roasted Sweet Chilli Chicken with Vegetable and Noodle Stir-Fry

Mix 500 g (1 lb) lean mini chicken fillets with 6 tablespoons sweet chilli sauce, 1 tablespoon soy sauce and 1 teaspoon each of powdered onion and garlic. Place the chicken mix on a nonstick baking tray and roast in a preheated oven, 200°C (400°F), Gas Mark 6, for 12–15 minutes until cooked through, turning once. Meanwhile, heat 2 teaspoons vegetable oil in a wok or frying pan over a medium heat. Add 400 g (13 oz) stir-fry

vegetables to the pan and cook for 2–3 minutes until beginning to wilt. Tip in 500 g (1 lb) fresh noodles and stir-fry for 3 minutes, then toss through 2 tablespoons light soy sauce and 1 tablespoon lime juice. Serve the chicken fillets with the stir-fry vegetables and noodles and extra sweet chilli dipping sauce on the side.

 # 20 'Meat Feast' Thin and Crispy Pizza

Serves 4

300 g (10 oz) thick passata
1 teaspoon lemon rind
pinch of sugar
1 teaspoon dried oregano
8 large, reduced-fat soft tortillas
100 g (3½ oz) wafer-thin slices of
 lean smoked ham, roughly sliced
100 g (3½ oz) wafer-thin slices
 lean turkey, roughly sliced
75 g (3 oz) thinly sliced bresaola,
 roughly chopped
8 thin slices pepper-coated
 pastrami, roughly chopped
125 g (4 oz) reduced-fat
 mozzarella cheese, cut into
 small dice
rocket leaves, to serve

· Preheat the oven to 200°C (400°F), Gas Mark 6. Put the passata, lemon rind, sugar and oregano in a saucepan over a medium-high heat. Season with salt and pepper, then bring almost to the boil. Reduce the heat and simmer gently for about 8 minutes or until thickened.

· Place 4 tortillas on a baking sheets, then spoon ½ tablespoon of the sauce evenly over each tortilla. Place a second tortilla on top of the sauce to sandwich the tortillas together.

· Spread the remaining sauce evenly over four doubled-up bases and top with a selection of the different meats. Scatter over the mozzarella and cook in the oven for 8–10 minutes until crisp and bubbling. Serve scattered with rocket leaves.

10 Super-Quick 'Meat Feast' Tortilla-Based Pizza Using 300 g (10 oz) ready-made Italian tomato sauce and 8 large, reduced-fat soft tortillas, make up the pizza bases on a large baking sheets as above. Sprinkle a 300 g (10 oz) selection of thinly sliced and roughly chopped, lean continental cooked meats over the bases, then scatter over 125 g (4 oz) grated reduced-fat Cheddar. Bake in a preheated oven, 200°C (400°F), Gas Mark 6, for 8–10 minutes until crisp and bubbling.

30 'Meat Feast' Italian Pizza Make the sauce as above. Meanwhile, combine 175 g (6 oz) wholemeal flour with 1 teaspoon each of fast-action yeast and caster sugar and ¾ teaspoon salt in a large bowl, making a well in the centre. Pour in 1½ tablespoons olive oil and 100 ml (3½ fl oz) hand-hot water, then knead the wet and dry ingredients together to make a smooth dough. Roll the dough out on a lightly floured surface so it is large enough to fit a large, nonstick baking sheet, then place the pizza base on the baking sheet. Using the tomato sauce and meat and mozzarella toppings as above, make up the pizza, then place in a preheated oven, 220°C (425°F), Gas Mark 7, for 12–15 minutes until crisp and bubbling.

30 Baked Chicken Parcels with Mozzarella and Basil

Serves 4

4 skinless chicken breasts, about 150 g (5 oz) each

4 teaspoons red chilli pesto or mild harissa

2 plum tomatoes, sliced

125 g (4 oz) reduced-fat mozzarella, cut into 8 slices

1 small bunch of basil, leaves stripped

8 thin slices of lean chorizo

To serve

500 g (1 lb) ready-made healthy couscous or bulgar wheat salad

rocket leaves

- Preheat the oven to 220°C (425°F), Gas Mark 7. Place the chicken breasts between 2 large sheets of clingfilm on a chopping board and beat with a rolling pin to flatten; they need to be about 4–5 mm (¼ inch) thick. Spread 1 teaspoon of the pesto or mild harissa evenly over each flattened chicken breast.

- Cover half of each chicken breast with 2–3 slices tomato and 2 slices mozzarella, then fold the uncovered half of the chicken over the filling to create a sandwich. Scatter the basil leaves over the top of the chicken parcels, reserving a few to garnish.

- Cover each parcel with 2 thin slices the chorizo, then secure with a wooden cocktail stick by threading it through the chicken breast. Place the parcels on a large, nonstick baking sheet, then cook in the oven for 15–18 minutes until cooked through.

- Serve the chicken parcels with the couscous or bulgar wheat salad, rocket leaves, garnished with the reserved basil leaves.

 Chicken and Tomato Salad with Pesto Dressing Slice 400 g (13 oz) cooked chicken fillets and arrange them on serving plates with 150 g (5 oz) rocket leaves, 2 tablespoons Parmesan cheese shavings and 200 g (7 oz) halved cherry tomatoes. Whisk 2 tablespoons pesto into 3 tablespoons aged balsamic vinegar and drizzle over the salad. Serve with warmed, sliced flatbreads.

 Grilled Chilli Pesto Chicken with Warm Couscous Salad Flatten 4 skinless chicken breasts, about 150 g (5 oz) each, as above, then spread 1 teaspoon chilli pesto evenly over each one. Place the chicken on a large, foil-lined baking sheet and slide under a preheated grill for 7–8 minutes until cooked through, turning once. Squeeze over the juice of 1 lemon and rest for 2–3 minutes before slicing thickly. Meanwhile, pour 350 ml (12 fl oz) boiling water over 225 g (7½ oz) dried, roasted vegetable or tomato couscous and stand for 5 minutes. Fluff up with a fork, then fold through 2 chopped plum tomatoes and 125 g (8 oz) diced reduced-fat mozzarella. Spoon the couscous on to serving plates, then scatter over the torn leaves from 1 small bunch of basil and 12 pimiento-stuffed olives. Arrange the sliced grilled chicken over the top of the couscous, drizzle over any juices from the chicken and serve.

30 Sweet and Spicy Pork with Red Peppers

Serves 4

1 tablespoon groundnut oil

1 onion, thickly sliced

2 long sweet red peppers, deseeded and diced

500 g (1 lb) pork tenderloin, cubed

1 teaspoon fennel seeds

1 teaspoon finely grated lemon rind

1–2 tablespoons nam prik pao (Thai chilli paste), to taste

¼ teaspoon chilli flakes (optional)

2 teaspoons tamarind paste

2 tablespoons sweet soy sauce or ketjap manis

400 g (13 oz) can chopped tomatoes

100 g (3½ oz) pineapple, peeled, 'eyes' removed, diced and lightly crushed

steamed rice, to serve

- Heat the oil in a large, heavy-based frying pan or flat-based wok over a medium heat, then add the onion and peppers and cook for 7–8 minutes or until softened, stirring occasionally.

- Add the pork and stir-fry for 1 minute to seal, then add the remaining ingredients and simmer for 12–15 minutes until the pork is cooked and the sauce thickened. Serve with steamed rice.

 Sweet and Sour Minced Pork and Pineapple Stir-Fry Heat 1 tablespoon groundnut oil in a large frying pan over a medium heat. Add 500 g (1 lb) lean minced pork and stir-fry for 5–6 minutes until cooked. Stir in 250 g (8 oz) sweet and sour sauce, 100 g (3½ oz) pineapple, diced and lightly crushed, and 200 g (7 oz) drained bamboo shoots. Simmer for 1–2 minutes until hot, then serve with steamed rice.

 Sweet and Sour Chicken Heat 1 tablespoon groundnut oil in a large, nonstick frying pan over a medium heat and stir 2 tablespoons cornflour into 1 tablespoon of water in a small bowl. Add 3 roughly chopped spring onions and 2 deseeded and diced long red peppers to the pan and stir-fry for 2–3 minutes. Tip in 400 g (13 oz) cubed skinless chicken breast and stir-fry for 2–3 minutes to seal, then add 100 g (3½ oz) pineapple, peeled, 'eyes' removed, diced and lightly crushed, 2 roughly chopped tomatoes, the cornflour mix, 200 ml (7 fl oz) pineapple juice, 1 tablespoon rice vinegar, 50 ml (2 fl oz) rice wine and 2 tablespoons each of soy sauce and tomato ketchup. Bring to the boil and simmer gently for 8–10 minutes until the chicken is cooked and the sauce thickened. Serve with steamed rice.

LOW-MEAT-BIG

 Honey and Mustard Glazed Chicken Fillets with Coleslaw

Serves 4

3 tablespoons clear honey

2 tablespoons wholegrain mustard

1 tablespoon Worcestershire sauce

1 tablespoon dark soy sauce

625 g (1¼ lb) skinless mini chicken fillets

mixed leaf salad, to serve

Coleslaw

½ red cabbage, shredded

½ small red onion, thinly sliced

1 large carrot, coarsely grated

4–6 tablespoons reduced-fat Caesar dressing

- Preheat the oven to 200°C (400°F), Gas Mark 6. Put the honey, mustard, Worcestershire sauce and soy sauce in a large bowl and mix to combine. Tip in the chicken fillets and toss until the chicken is well coated in the glaze.

- Scrape the chicken into a foil-lined roasting tin, spread out over the base and then put in the oven for about 15 minutes, turning once, until cooked through.

- Meanwhile, to make the coleslaw, combine the cabbage, red onion and carrot in a large bowl, then mix with 4–6 tablespoons of the Caesar dressing, depending on the consistency desired.

- Serve the glazed fillets on top of a mixed leaf salad together with the coleslaw.

 Honey and Mustard Chicken Slaw Salad
To make a honey and mustard dressing, combine 1 tablespoon honey, 1 tablespoon wholegrain mustard, 1½ tablespoons Worcestershire sauce, 2 teaspoons dark soy and 2–3 tablespoons freshly squeezed orange juice in a jug or bowl. In a large bowl, toss together 400 g (13 oz) cooked mini chicken fillets, ½ shredded red cabbage, ½ thinly sliced small red onion and 1 coarsely grated large carrot. Arrange the chicken and cabbage salad on serving plates, scatter with 150 g (5 oz) baked croutons and drizzle over the dressing. Serve immediately.

 Baked Jerk and Mustard Chicken and Coleslaw Cut 3–4 deep slashes in 4 skinless free-range skinless chicken breasts, about 150 g (5 oz) each, and place on a foil-lined baking tray. Mix together 3 tablespoons honey, 2 tablespoons wholegrain mustard, 2 teaspoons jerk seasoning mix and 1 finely chopped garlic clove. Massage the marinade into the chicken and put in a preheated oven, 200°C (400°F), Gas Mark 6, for 20–25 minutes until cooked through. Meanwhile, make the coleslaw as above. Serve the baked chicken breasts with the coleslaw and ½ a baked potato per person.

30 Chinese 5-Spice Duck with Ramen Noodles

Serves 4

1 teaspoon Chinese 5-spice powder
1 tablespoon clear honey
2 tablespoons ketjap manis or sweet soy sauce
2 large duck breasts, about 450 g (1 lb) each, skin removed
1 litre (1¾ pints) clear chicken stock
1 garlic clove, thinly sliced
1 tablespoon finely chopped fresh root ginger
2 spring onions, sliced diagonally
150 g (5 oz) drained bamboo shoots
200 g (7 oz) bean sprouts
350 g (11½ oz) ramen noodles or medium egg noodles
2 teaspoons toasted sesame seeds, to serve

- Preheat the oven 220°C (425°F), Gas Mark 7. Put the Chinese 5-spice powder, honey and 1 tablespoon of the ketjap manis in a bowl and mix. Take the duck breasts and score with a sharp knife. Rub the 5-spice mixture into the duck all over and set aside for 5 minutes.

- Heat a frying pan, add the duck breasts, spice side down, and cook for 5–7 minutes until golden. Turn them over and cook for a further 2–3 minutes, then transfer to a small roasting tin and put in the oven for 5–10 minutes until cooked as desired.

- Meanwhile, put the stock, remaining ketjap manis, garlic and ginger in a saucepan over a medium heat and bring to a gentle boil. Reduce the heat and simmer for 10 minutes, then add the spring onions and bamboo shoots. Simmer for a further 2 minutes, then stir in the bean sprouts.

- In a separate saucepan cook the noodles in boiling water for 2–3 minutes, or according to the packet instructions. Drain into a colander. Remove the duck from the oven, leave to rest for 2–3 minutes and slice thinly. Ladle the soup into deep bowls. Divide the noodles between the bowls, then arrange the sliced duck on top. Sprinkle with sesame seeds and serve.

10 Quick Chinese 5-Spice Noodle Soup

Put 1 litre (1¾ pints) vegetable stock, 1 teaspoon Chinese 5 spice paste, 2 tablespoons ketjap manis and 1 teaspoon each of finely chopped garlic and fresh root ginger in a saucepan over a medium-high heat and bring up to a gentle boil. Reduce the heat and simmer for 5–7 minutes. Meanwhile, diagonally slice 2 spring onions and cut 200 g (7 oz) firm tofu into slices.

Reheat 450 g (14½ oz) straight-to-wok medium noodles, according to the packet instructions, and heap the noodles into deep bowls. Top the noodles with 200 g (7 oz) bean sprouts and the tofu slices, then sprinkle with the spring onions. Ladle over the hot soup and serve.

20 Duck and Egg Noodle Stir-Fry

Thinly slice 450 g (14½ oz) duck fillets. Heat 2 teaspoons vegetable oil in a wok over a medium heat, add 1 thinly sliced garlic clove, 1 tablespoon finely chopped ginger and 2 sliced spring onions, and stir-fry for 30 seconds. Add the duck and 500 g (1 lb) fresh egg noodles and stir-fry for 3 minutes. Stir in 300 g (10 oz) Chinese-style stir-fry sauce and simmer for 1 minute before serving.

30 Mild and Creamy Chicken Curry

Serves 4

1½ tablespoons groundnut oil
1 large onion, sliced
2 garlic cloves, finely chopped
1 teaspoon ground turmeric
1 teaspoon ground cumin
1 teaspoon ground coriander
150 g (5 oz) korma paste
500 g (1 lb) skinless chicken breast, cubed
250 g (8 oz) sweet potato, peeled and cubed
200 ml (7 fl oz) reduced-fat coconut milk
100 ml (3½ fl oz) water
2 tablespoons ground almonds
250 g (8 oz) basmati rice, washed
2 tablespoons chopped coriander leaves, to garnish
low-fat naan bread, to serve (optional)

- Heat the oil in a saucepan or deep frying pan over a medium heat, then add the onion and cook for 5–6 minutes until softened, stirring frequently.

- Add the garlic, spices and korma paste and stir-fry for 1–2 minutes, then stir in the chicken and sweet potato. Cook for 3–4 minutes to seal the chicken, then add the coconut milk, water and ground almonds and season with salt and pepper. Bring to the boil, then reduce the heat and simmer gently for 12–15 minutes until the chicken is cooked and the potato is tender.

- Meanwhile, put the basmati rice in a large pan of lightly salted boiling water and cook for 12 minutes until tender, or according to the packet instructions.

- Serve the curry on a bed of rice, garnished with the coriander and with naan bread on the side, if liked.

10 Cold Chicken Curry Salad with Rice

Mix together 200 g (7 oz) fat-free Greek yogurt, 100 g (3½ oz) extra-light mayonnaise, 1 teaspoon curry powder, 3 tablespoons smooth mango chutney, 2 teaspoons lemon juice and 2 tablespoons chopped coriander in a large bowl. Roughly slice 400 g (13 oz) tikka roasted chicken mini fillets, then fold into the curry mayonnaise sauce. Serve with 400 g (13 oz) cold, steamed wild basmati rice and lemon wedges.

20 Grilled Korma Chicken with Rice

Cut 3–4 deep slashes in 4 skinless free-range chicken breasts, about 150 g (5 oz) each, then cover each breast with 1 tablespoon korma paste. Place the chicken on a foil-lined baking sheet and slide under a preheated grill for 12–15 minutes until cooked, turning once. Serve with 500 g (1 lb) ready-cooked basmati rice, topped with a couple of dollops fat-free natural yogurt and with lemon wedges on the side.

30 Lebanese-Spiced Lamb Skewers with Cucumber Salad

Serves 4

500 g (1 lb) lean minced lamb
½ teaspoon ground nutmeg
½ teaspoon ground ginger
½ teaspoon ground allspice
½ teaspoon ground black pepper
½ teaspoon ground cinnamon
½ teaspoon ground cloves
1 garlic clove, finely chopped
2 tablespoons chopped mint
finely grated rind of 1 lemon
salt and pepper
1–2 teaspoons sumac, (optional)

Cucumber salad

1 cucumber, deseeded and finely
  chopped
1 green pepper, deseeded and
  finely chopped
1 large bunch finely chopped parsley
1 large bunch finely chopped mint
3 tomatoes, deseeded and finely
  chopped
juice of 1 lemon

- Put the minced lamb, ground spices, garlic, mint, lemon rind and 1 tablespoon of the lemon juice from the cucumber salad in a large bowl. Season generously with salt and pepper, then mix all the ingredients together until well combined. Mould the spiced mince into 8 slightly flattened sausage shapes, then thread 2 sausages each on to 4 long metal skewers. Set aside.

- Meanwhile, to make the cucumber salad, mix together the cucumber, pepper, parsley, mint and tomatoes in a bowl. Season generously with salt and pepper, then stir in the remaining lemon juice. Set aside.

- Place the lamb skewers on a grill rack, then slide under a preheated grill for 6–7 minutes, turning once, until cooked through and browned all over.

- Arrange the salad on to serving plates, then place the lamb skewers on the salad. Sprinkle over the sumac, if using, and serve with griddled pitta bread and lemon wedges, if liked.

10 Baharat Spiced Lamb and Couscous

Mix 3 teaspoons baharat spice mix (or mix together the ground spices above) with 2 tablespoons each of lemon juice and chopped mint. Rub over 4 lean lamb steaks, about 125 g (4 oz) each, and place under a preheated grill for 4–6 minutes or until cooked, turning once. Serve with quick-cook lemon and garlic couscous.

20 Chawarma-Style Pitta Lamb Kebabs

Mix together 3 teaspoons baharat spice mix (or mix together the above ground spices) and 2 tablespoons each of lemon juice and chopped mint in a bowl. Rub the marinade over 4 lean lamb steaks, about 125 g (4 oz) each, and place under a preheated grill for 4–6 minutes or until cooked to your liking,

turning once. Meanwhile, make the cucumber salad as above. Slice the lamb thinly and stuff inside 4 large, warmed pittas. Spoon the cucumber salad into the pittas, then drizzle 3–4 tablespoons garlicky yogurt or tahini dressing over the salad. Serve sprinkled with 1–2 teaspoons sumac, if liked.

 # Chinese Pork and Vegetables

Serves 4

2 tablespoons clear honey

2 tablespoons dark soy sauce

2 teaspoons Chinese 5-spice powder

1 teaspoon Szechuan pepper, lightly crushed

1 teaspoon finely grated fresh root ginger

2 teaspoons sesame oil

500 g (1 lb) pork tenderloin, thickly sliced

1 red pepper, deseeded and thinly sliced

500 g (1 lb) Chinese cabbage or Chinese leaf, thinly sliced

200 g (7 oz) bean sprouts

200 g (7 oz) baby pak choi, cut in half lengthways

2 teaspoons sesame seeds, to serve

- Mix together the honey, soy sauce, Chinese 5 spice powder, Szechuan pepper, ginger and 1 teaspoon of the sesame oil in a bowl. Tip the pork into the bowl and massage the meat well with the marinade.

- Heat a large, nonstick frying pan over a medium-high heat, then scrape the pork mixture into the pan and cook for 4–5 minutes, turning occasionally, until the pork is just cooked and tender.

- Meanwhile, heat the remaining 1 teaspoon sesame oil in a wok over a medium-high heat, then add the red pepper, Chinese cabbage or Chinese leaf, bean sprouts and baby pak choi and stir-fry for 2–3 minutes until just tender.

- Remove the pork from the heat and serve immediately with the stir-fried vegetables and sprinkled with sesame seeds.

Minced Pork and Little Gem Stir-Fry

Heat 2 teaspoons sesame oil in a large frying pan over a medium heat, add 500 g (1 lb) lean minced pork and stir-fry for 5–6 minutes until cooked and browned. Stir in 2 tablespoons each of clear honey and dark soy sauce, 2 teaspoons Chinese 5-spice power and 1 teaspoon each of Szechuan peppercorns and grated fresh root ginger. Cook for a further 1–2 minutes, then serve with whole Little Gem lettuce leaves.

Chinese-Style Traybake

Tip 1 deseeded and thinly sliced red pepper, 500 g (1 lb) thinly sliced Chinese cabbage or Chinese leaf, 200 g (7 oz) bean sprouts and 200 g (7 oz) baby pak choi, cut in half lengthways, into a large nonstick roasting tin. In a large bowl mix together 2 tablespoons each clear honey and dark soy sauce, 2 teaspoons Chinese 5 spice powder, 1 teaspoon Szechuan pepper, lightly crushed, 1 teaspoon finely grated fresh root ginger and 2 teaspoons sesame oil. Tip 500 g (1 lb) thickly sliced pork tenderloin into the marinade and toss until the pork is well coated. Scatter the pork evenly over the vegetables, and put the vegetables and pork in a preheated oven, 220°C (425°F), Gas Mark 7, for 18–20 minutes until just cooked and tender. Serve sprinkled with 2 teaspoons sesame seeds.

20 Baked Gnocchi with Smoked Turkey and Blue Cheese

Serves 4

750 g (1½ lb) fresh gnocchi
200 g (7 oz) quark cheese or extra-light cream cheese
125 g (4 oz) strong blue cheese, such as Gorgonzola piccante or Stilton
2 tablespoons snipped chives
200 g (7 oz) cooked smoked turkey, cut into strips
200 g (7 oz) frozen chopped spinach, defrosted
2 spring onions, trimmed and thinly sliced
black pepper

- Preheat the oven to 220°C (425°F), Gas Mark 7. Bring a large saucepan of lightly salted water to the boil and cook the gnocchi for 2 minutes until cooked through, or according to the packet instructions. Drain well, then tip back into the saucepan.

- Meanwhile, gently warm the quark or cream cheese, blue cheese and chives in a frying pan, then season with pepper. Remove from the heat, stir in the smoked turkey and spinach and gently fold the sauce into the cooked gnocchi.

- Scrape the gnocchi and sauce into an ovenproof dish, scatter with the spring onions and place in the oven for 15–18 minutes until golden and bubbling.

- Serve the baked gnocchi with a crisp green leaf salad and crusty bread, if liked.

10 Baby Gnocchi with Creamy Blue Cheese and Turkey Sauce

Cook 750 g (1½ lb) tricolour baby gnocchi as above. Drain and spoon into deep bowls. Meanwhile, melt 125 g (4 oz) Gorgonzola Piccante, with 280 ml (9½ fl oz) low-fat single cream in a pan over a low heat, stirring. Stir in 2 tablespoons snipped chives and season with black pepper. Simmer for 1–2 minutes, take off the heat and stir in 200 g (7 oz) cooked smoked turkey, cut into strips. Pour the sauce over the gnocchi and serve with sliced spring onions.

30 Gnocchi, Squash, Sweet Potato and Blue Cheese Bake

Chop 400 g (10 oz) each butternut squash and sweet potato into a saucepan of lightly salted boiling water. Cook for 15 minutes or until tender. Drain into a colander, then tip back into the saucepan and crush slightly with a fork. Meanwhile, make the smoked turkey and blue cheese sauce as above, then cook 500 g (1 lb) potato gnocchi or tricolour baby gnocchi in a large saucepan of lightly salted boiling water for 2 minutes, or according to the packet instructions. Mix the gnocchi through the sauce, then fold through the crushed butternut squash and sweet potato. Scrape all the ingredients into an ovenproof dish, sprinkle over 2 trimmed and sliced spring onions and bake in a preheated oven, 230°C (450°F), Gas Mark 8, for 12 minutes until bubbling. Serve with a green salad.

Fast-Seared Steak with French Beans

Serves 4

400 g (13 oz) green beans, trimmed
1 teaspoon olive ol
4 thin steaks, such as feather steaks or frying steaks
200 g (7 oz) peppery rocket salad
salt and pepper
crusty baguette, to serve

Tomato dressing

2 tomatoes, diced
1 teaspoon olive oil
1 banana shallot, finely chopped
1 tablespoon wholegrain mustard
1 tablespoon red wine vinegar

- Bring a saucepan of lightly salted water to the boil, then add the green beans and cook for 2–3 minutes until tender but firm.

- Meanwhile, to make the tomato dressing, put the tomatoes, oil, shallot, mustard and red wine vinegar in a bowl and mix to combine.

- Drain the beans and return to the pan. Toss the tomato dressing through the beans, season generously with salt and pepper, cover and keep warm.

- Heat a large ridged griddle pan over a high heat. Rub the oil over the steaks, then cook the steaks in the griddle pan for 1 minute each side. Remove and rest for 1–2 minutes.

- Divide the peppery rocket salad on to serving plates. Spoon the beans and their dressing over the beans, then top each plate with a seared steak. Serve immediately with crusty French baguette.

 Peppered Steak with Wilted Spinach, Capers and Tomatoes
Heat 2 teaspoons olive oil in small frying pan over a medium heat. Add 1 finely sliced banana shallot and 2 finely chopped garlic cloves and cook for 5–6 minutes until softened, stirring occasionally. Add 4 deseeded and chopped tomatoes, 1½ tablespoons rinsed capers and 1 tablespoon red wine vinegar. Cook gently for 2–3 minutes to heat through, then stir in 200 g (7 oz) spinach leaves until just wilted. Meanwhile, rub 1 teaspoon olive oil over 4 lean rump steaks, about 150 g (5 oz) each. Coat the steaks generously in coarsely ground black pepper and place on a hot griddle pan over a medium-high heat. Cook the steaks for 2–3 minutes each side. Meanwhile cook 400 g (13 oz) trimmed green beans in boiling water for 2–3 minutes until tender. Serve the beans with the warmed tomato and spinach and peppered steak.

Pan-Fried Steak with New Potatoes and Rocket Salad Cook 500 g (1 lb) halved baby new potatoes, in 500 ml (17 fl oz) vegetable stock, or enough stock to just cover the potatoes. Cover the pan with foil and a lid and simmer for 15–18 minutes until tender. Meanwhile, make the tomato dressing, as above. Rub 4 fillet steaks, about 150 g (5 oz) each, with 1 teaspoon olive oil and season with salt and pepper. Cook as above for 2–4 minutes each side. Serve with the potatoes and 200 g (7 oz) rocket tossed with the tomato dressing.

30 Crispy Garlic Baked Stuffed Chicken Breasts

Serves 4

4 free-range skinless chicken breasts, about 150 g (5 oz) each
100 g (3½ oz) low-fat cream cheese
1 large garlic clove, finely chopped
2 tablespoons chopped parsley
½ tablespoon lemon juice
1 teaspoon finely grated lemon rind
75 g (3 oz) plain flour
1 large egg, beaten
75 g (3 oz) dried white breadcrumbs
salt and pepper

To serve

500 g (1 lb) new potatoes
350 g (11½ oz) broccoli florets

- Preheat the oven to 220°C (425°F), Gas Mark 7. Cut deep slits along the sides of the chicken breasts to create a pocket in each. Mix together the cream cheese, garlic, parsley and lemon juice and rind. Season well with salt and pepper, then spoon the filling into the chicken.

- Place the flour, egg and breadcrumbs in separate shallow dishes. Coat each chicken breast first in the flour, then the egg and then the breadcrumbs and place on a baking tray. Cook the chicken in the oven for 15–18 minutes until cooked.

- Meanwhile, cook the new potatoes in a saucepan of lightly salted boiling water for 15–18 minutes until tender.

- Cook the broccoli florets in a large basket steamer for 3–4 minutes until tender. Alternatively, cook in an electric steamer, according to the manufacturer's instructions.

- Serve the crisp baked chicken with the broccoli and new potatoes.

10 Garlicky Cream Cheese and Chicken Rolls

Cut 4 ciabatta-style rolls in half and toast, cut side down, on a ridged griddle pan over a medium heat until golden and nicely charred. Rub the toasted sides of the rolls with the cut sides of 1 garlic clove, then spread the bases with 100 g (3½ oz) low-fat cream cheese. Scatter over 75 g (3 oz) baby leaf salad leaves, then top with 300 g (10 oz) cooked chicken slices. Squeeze over a little lemon juice and top the bases with the other half of the rolls.

20 Chicken Fillets in Garlic and Herb Breadcrumbs

Mix together 75 g (3 oz) dried white breadcrumbs with 1 teaspoon each of garlic powder and dried herbes de Provence in a shallow dish. Put 75 g (3 oz) plain flour in a separate dish and 1 beaten egg in another dish. Coat 500 g (1 lb) skinless mini chicken fillets in the flour, then the egg, then in breadcrumbs, and place on a baking tray. Put in a preheated oven, 220°C (425°F), Gas Mark 7, for 12–15 minutes until cooked, then serve with mashed potatoes and a mixed leaf salad.

LOW-MEAT-QUW

Moroccan Grilled Lamb with Sultanas

Serves 4

450 ml (¾ pint) lamb stock
75 g (3 oz) sultanas
1 large preserved lemon, chopped
4 lean lamb fillets, about 150 g (5 oz) each
350 g (11½ oz) couscous
1 teaspoon olive oil
1–2 tablespoons toasted flaked almonds, to garnish

Spicy yogurt paste

2 garlic cloves, finely chopped
2 tablespoons finely chopped mint, plus extra leaves to garnish
1 teaspoon ground coriander
1 teaspoon ground cumin
¼ teaspoon ground ginger
1 tablespoon lemon juice
6 tablespoons natural yogurt
½ teaspoon harissa

- Pour the lamb stock into a saucepan over a low heat, add the sultanas and preserved lemon and heat to an almost simmer. Cover and keep warm.

- Make the spicy yogurt paste by mixing together all the ingredients in a small bowl. Add more harissa, if liked.

- Slice the lamb fillets in half lengthways, without quite cutting all the way through. Open up the fillets like a butterfly and massage the spice paste into the meat.

- Place the couscous, olive oil and a pinch of salt in a large bowl and mix until all the grains are coated in the oil. Stir in the hot lamb stock with the sultanas and preserved lemon, then cover and set aside in a warm place for 12–15 minutes until the couscous is tender and the liquid has been absorbed.

- Meanwhile, cook the lamb fillets under a preheated grill for 6–8 minutes, turning once, or until cooked as desired. Leave to rest covered loosely with foil. Heap the couscous onto serving plates, scatter over the mint leaves and top with the lamb. Scatter over the toasted almonds and serve.

 Moroccan-Spiced Lamb with Couscous

Make the spicy yogurt paste as above, then rub over 4 lean lamb steaks, about 125 g (4 oz) each. Grill the lamb for 2–3 minutes each side or as desired. Meanwhile, put 75 g (3 oz) raisins in a small pan, cover with boiling water and simmer for 3–4 minutes to swell. Serve the lamb with 500 g (1 lb) low-fat, ready-made roasted vegetable couscous salad, top with the drained raisins and 1–2 tablespoons toasted flaked almonds.

 Moroccan Lamb Skewers with Preserved Lemon Couscous

Make the spicy yogurt paste in a large bowl as above. Cut 500 g (1 lb) lean lamb leg meat into cubes, tip into the paste and mix until coated. Set aside to marinate for 10 minutes. Meanwhile, place 350 g (11½ oz) couscous in a large bowl with 1 teaspoon olive oil and a pinch of salt and mix until the grains are coated in the oil. Stir in 450 ml (¾ pint) hot lamb stock, 75 g (3 oz) sultanas and 1 chopped large preserved lemon. Cover and set aside in a warm place for 12–15 minutes until all the liquid has been absorbed. Cut 2 courgettes and 1 red onion into chunks and thread on to 4 metal skewers with the lamb. Place the skewers under a preheated grill for 7–8 minutes or until cooked as desired, turning frequently. Serve the skewers with the couscous. Scatter over toasted flaked almonds, if liked.

 # Quick Beef Bolognaise

Serves 4

1 onion, roughly chopped
1 carrot, roughly chopped
1 celery stick, trimmed and roughly chopped
1 large field mushroom, about 100 g (3½ oz), roughly chopped
1 tablespoon olive oil
2 garlic cloves, finely chopped
350 g (11½ oz) lean beef mince
400 g (13 oz) spaghetti
300 g (10 oz) low-fat, Italian-style fresh tomato sauce for pasta
300 ml (½ pint) boiling water
½ teaspoon finely grated lemon rind
½ teaspoon dried oregano
4 teaspoons grated Parmesan cheese, to serve (optional)
salt and pepper

- Put the onion, carrots, celery and mushroom in a food processor or blender and pulse until finely chopped.

- Heat the olive oil in a large, deep-sided frying pan over medium heat, tip in the chopped vegetables and cook for 3 minutes, stirring occasionally. Add the garlic and cook for 2–3 minutes until softened, stirring frequently. Tip in the minced beef, increase the heat to high and cook for 2–3 minutes until browned.

- Meanwhile, bring a large saucepan of lightly salted water to the boil and cook the spaghetti for 11 minutes until 'al dente', or according to the packet instructions.

- Pour the tomato sauce for pasta into the pan with the meat with the measured boiling water, lemon rind and oregano. Season with salt and pepper, reduce the heat, cover loosely and simmer for about 10 minutes, or until thickened.

- Drain the pasta and serve in deep bowls topped with the bolognaise sauce and a little grated Parmesan, if liked.

 Minced Beef and Tomato Spaghetti
Heat 1 tablespoon olive oil in a large, nonstick frying pan over a medium heat, add 500 g (1 lb) lean minced beef and cook for 5–6 minutes until browned and cooked. Stir 750 g (1¼ lb) fresh tomato-based pasta sauce into the meat and stir to reheat. Serve with 500 g (1 lb) cooked fresh spaghetti.

 Penne Bolognaise Bake Cook 300 g (10 oz) penne in lightly salted boiling water for about 10 minutes until 'al dente', or according to the packet instructions. Make the quick beef bolognaise as above, then stir into the drained pasta. Scrape into an ovenproof dish, sprinkle over 2 tablespoons grated Parmesan cheese and place in a preheated oven, 230°C (450°F), Gas Mark 8, for 8–10 minutes until bubbling.

LOW-MEAT-SOC

30 Roast Pork Tenderloin with Lemon, Sage and Capers

Serves 4

2 thin pork tenderloins, about 300 g (10 oz) each, cut in half
1 garlic clove, roughly chopped
1 tablespoon chopped sage leaves
finely grated rind and juice of 1 lemon
4 teaspoons olive oil
2 teaspoons clear honey
1 tablespoon capers, rinsed and drained
2 long banana shallots, chopped
300 g (10 oz) baby leaf spinach, roughly sliced
8–12 caperberries, to garnish
salt and pepper

· Preheat the oven to 220°C (425°F), Gas Mark 7. Slice the pork tenderloin lengthways without quite cutting all the way through and open up like a butterfly.

· Place the garlic, sage, lemon rind, 2 teaspoons olive oil, honey, capers and 1 teaspoon of lemon juice in a mini chopper and blend to a rough paste. Rub the mixture all over the pork.

· Heat a frying pan over a medium heat, add the pork and fry for 1 minute to seal, turning once. Transfer the pork to a small roasting tin, season with salt and pepper and roast in the oven for 10 minutes or until cooked and the juices run clear. Remove from the oven, cover with foil and set aside to rest.

· Meanwhile, heat the remaining oil in a frying pan over a low heat, add the shallots and cook for 5–6 minutes until softened. Add the spinach leaves to the pan and stir until wilted. Stir in the remaining lemon juice, season with salt and pepper, then spoon on to serving plates. Place the pork on top and scatter over caperberries to serve.

10 Pan-Fried Pork with Lemon, Sage and Honey Dressing

Cut in half 2 thin pork tenderloins, about 300 g (10 oz) each, and place between 2 sheets of clingfilm. Batter the tenderloins with a rolling pin to flatten and season with salt and pepper. Heat 2 teaspoons olive oil in a frying pan over a medium heat, add the tenderloin and fry for 1–2 minutes each side until browned and cooked through. Cover the tenderloins with foil and set aside to rest.

Meanwhile, make a dressing by combining 2 tablespoons olive oil, the juice of 1 lemon, 1 tablespoon chopped sage leaves and 1 teaspoon clear honey. Mix any juices from the cooked tenderloins into the dressing, then pour the dressing over the pork slices and serve with 175 (6 oz) baby spinach leaves.

20 Pork Medallions with Lemon and Caper Sauce

Slice 2 thin pork tenderloins, about 300 g (10 oz) each, into 1.5 cm (¾ inch) medallions. Heat 4 teaspoons olive oil in a frying pan and cook the pork for 1–2 minutes on each side. Add 1 chopped garlic clove, finely grated rind of 1 lemon, 1 tablespoon each of chopped sage leaves and capers, 2 teaspoons clear honey and 200 ml (7 fl oz) dry white wine and simmer for 2–3 minutes until the pork is cooked. Serve with wilted spinach as above.

20 Serrano Ham and Watercress Salad with Avocado

Serves 4

1 long granary or multigrain
baguette, cut into large cubes

1 tablespoon avocado oil, plus
extra to serve (optional)

125 g (4 oz) watercress leaves

8 thin Serrano ham slices

4 plum tomatoes, sliced

2 ripe but firm Hass avocados,
peeled, stoned and sliced

3–4 teaspoons raspberry vinegar,
plus extra to serve (optional)

50 g (2 oz) walnuts pieces
(optional)

salt and pepper

- Preheat the oven to 180 °C (350 °F), Gas Mark 4. Scatter the baguette cubes over a large baking sheet, drizzle with avocado oil and season with salt. Cook the cubes in the oven for 10–12 minutes until crisp and golden. Remove from the oven and set aside to cool.

- Put the watercress leaves on to serving plates and arrange the slices of ham, tomato and avocado over them. Scatter over the cooled croutons, then drizzle with raspberry vinegar, to taste, and season generously with pepper.

- Scatter with the walnuts, if using, and serve drizzled with a little extra avocado oil and raspberry vinegar, if liked.

---

10 Avocado, Serrano Ham and Watercress Open Sandwiches

Crush together 2 ripe avocados, 1 teaspoon raspberry vinegar and 50 g (2 oz) walnut pieces in a bowl and season with salt and pepper. Slice open 4 small crusty granary baguettes, then spread the avocado mixture over the bases and scatter with 125 g (4 oz) watercress leaves. Layer 2 thin slices Serrano ham over each baguette. Serve as open sandwiches, drizzled with avocado oil and seasoned with cracked black pepper.

30 Warmed Roasted Tomato and Serrano Ham Pasta

Place 500 g mixed red and yellow cherry tomatoes in a nonstick roasting tin, sprinkle with 2 finely sliced garlic cloves and 2 tablespoons olive oil and season generously with salt and pepper. Roast the tomatoes in a preheated oven, 180 °C (350 °F), Gas Mark 4, for about 25 minutes or until cooked and beginning to burst. Meanwhile, cook 350 g (11½ oz) tricolour pasta in lightly salted boiling water for 11 minutes until 'al dente', or according to the

packet instructions. Drain the pasta into a colander and cool under running cold water, then tip into a bowl and toss with 3–4 tablespoons raspberry vinegar, to taste, 8 thin slices of Serrano ham, cut into strips, and 50 g (2 oz) walnut pieces. Add the roasted tomatoes to the bowl and toss gently through the pasta. Serve warm with a watercress and avocado salad as a side dish.

30 Stuffed Pork Steaks with Butter Bean Salad

Serves 4

4 thick lean pork loin steaks,
about 200 g (7 oz) each
1½ tablespoons olive oil
2 garlic cloves, finely chopped
finely grated rind of 1 lemon
1 teaspoon fennel seeds
125 g (4 oz) light mozzarella
125 ml (4 fl oz) dry white wine
salt and pepper

Bean salad

1½ tablespoons olive oil
1 red onion, finely sliced
2 teaspoons fennel seeds
400 g (13 oz) can butter beans
75 g (3 oz) pitted kalamata olives,
roughly chopped
300 g (10 oz) sweet baby plum
tomatoes, cut into quarters
8 slow-roasted, ready-to-eat
tomatoes, chopped
1 small bunch of basil, chopped
175 g (6 oz) roasted red peppers
2 tablespoons lemon juice

- Preheat the oven to 220°C (425°F), Gas Mark 7. Cut slits along the sides of the pork loin steaks to create a pocket in each. Mix together the olive oil, garlic, lemon rind, fennel seeds and pepper, to taste, in a small bowl. Rub the mixture all over the steaks, including inside the pockets, slice the mozzarella into 8 and stuff 2 slices inside each pocket.

- Heat a large, nonstick frying pan over a medium-high heat, add the pork steaks and fry for 1–2 minutes each side until golden. Pour the white wine over the steaks and bring up to the boil. Remove the pan from the heat and transfer the pork to a snug-fitting ovenproof dish. Pour over the wine and juices and put in the oven for about 15 minutes or until just cooked through and tender.

- Meanwhile, to make the bean salad, heat the olive oil in a clean frying pan over a medium-low heat, add the onion and fennel seeds and cook for 7–8 minutes until softened, stirring occasionally. Drain the beans and add with the olives, tomatoes, basil and roasted peppers to the pan, season with salt and pepper and heat until the salad is warm. Stir through the lemon juice, then spoon on to serving plates.

- Top each plate of bean salad with a pork steak, drizzle over any juices remaining in the pan and serve immediately.

 Bean Salad with Mozzarella and Parma Ham Mix 400 g (13 oz) can butter beans, drained, with 300 g (10 oz) sweet baby plum tomatoes, cut into quarters, 75 g (3 oz) roughly chopped pitted kalamata olives, 8 chopped slow-roasted, ready-to-eat tomatoes, 2 teaspoons fennel seeds, ½ tea-

spoon olive oil and 2 tablespoons lemon juice in a bowl until well combined. Spoon the bean salad on to serving plates, then tear 125 g (4 oz) light mozzarella cheese into pieces and scatter over the salads. Toss 125 g (4 oz) wild rocket leaves and 2 thin slices lean Parma ham through each plate of bean salad and mozzarella and serve.

 Grilled Pork with Bean Salad In a small bowl mix 2 teaspoons fennel seeds, the grated rind of 1 lemon, 2 finely chopped garlic cloves and pepper to taste. Rub over 4 lean pork steaks and grill for 6–8 minutes until golden and cooked through, turning once. Serve with the bean salad as above.

30 Chicken Risotto with White Wine and Asparagus

Serves 4

1½ tablespoons extra virgin
  rapeseed oil
1 small onion, finely chopped
250 g (8 oz) lean boneless,
  skinless chicken thigh, diced
300 g (10 oz) risotto rice
200 ml (7 fl oz) dry white wine
1 litre (1¾ pints) hot chicken stock
250 g (8 oz) asparagus stalks,
  trimmed
2 tablespoons reduced-fat
  mascarpone cheese
pepper

- Heat the oil in a large, deep-sided frying pan over a medium-high heat, then add the onion and cook for 4–5 minutes until softened, stirring occasionally. Add the chicken and stir-fry for 2 minutes until browned.

- Stir in the rice, then pour in the dry white wine and simmer rapidly, stirring constantly, until the liquid has been absorbed.

- Reduce the heat, add a small ladleful of the hot chicken stock and stir constantly at a gentle simmer until the stock has been absorbed. Repeat this process until all the stock has been absorbed and the rice is 'al dente' – about 17 minutes.

- Stir the mascarpone into the rice, cover the pan with a lid and set aside to rest for 2–3 minutes.

- Meanwhile, place the asparagus stalks in a basket steamer and cook for 2–3 minutes until tender.

- Spoon the risotto on to serving plates, season with pepper and serve with the asparagus.

1 Creamy Rice with Chicken and Mushrooms Fry 200 g (7 oz) chopped brown cap mushrooms in 1½ tablespoons extra virgin rapeseed oil over a medium-high heat for 3–4 minutes, then pour in 125 ml (4 fl oz) vermouth and 300 g (10 oz) roughly chopped, cooked chicken. Simmer rapidly to evaporate the vermouth, then stir in 250 ml (8 fl oz) hot chicken stock, 2 tablespoons reduced-fat mascarpone and 400 g (13 oz) cooked long grain rice. Season with salt and pepper and serve.

2 Chicken, Mushroom and Asparagus Risotto Pour 900 ml (1½ pints) chicken or vegetable stock into a saucepan and heat to a gentle boil. Fry 1 finely chopped small onion in 1½ tablespoons extra virgin rapeseed oil over a medium-high heat for 3–4 minutes, then add 250 g (8 oz) diced lean, boneless, skinlesss chicken thigh and stir-fry to brown the meat. Pour in 200 ml (7 fl oz) dry white wine and simmer rapidly to evaporate, then stir in 2 x 175 g (6 oz) packets of quick-cook

mushroom risotto. Add the boiling stock and simmer gently for 12 minutes until 'al dente', stirring occasionally. Meanwhile, place 250 g (8 oz) trimmed asparagus stalks in a basket steamer and lower into a shallow pan of simmering water so that the basket does not quite touch the surface of the water. Cook for 2–3 minutes until tender. Stir 2 tablespoons reduced-fat mascarpone into the risotto, if liked, then serve the risotto in deep bowls topped with the asparagus.

30 Poached Poussin with Baby Vegetables

Serves 4

2 poussins, about 450 g (14½ oz) each, cut in half lengthways

200 g (7 oz) baby courgettes, cut in half lengthways

200 g (7 oz) baby carrots, cut in half lengthways

150 g (5 oz) baby leeks, cut in half lengthways

1–1½ litres (1¾–2½ pints) good quality chicken stock

1 bouquet garni made with fresh parsley, bay leaves and thyme

125 g (4 oz) fine asparagus tips, trimmed

1 baby green cabbage, cut into thin wedges

salt and pepper

- Place the poussins in a large, heavy-based casserole with the baby vegetables, asparagus and cabbage and enough chicken stock to almost cover the poussins. Add the bouquet garni, then place the casserole over a high heat and bring to the boil. Reduce the heat and simmer gently for 15–18 minutes until the poussins are cooked and the vegetables tender. Season with salt and pepper.

- Remove the bouquet garni from the casserole and peel the skins off from the poussins. Serve the poussin in deep dishes with the vegetables and plenty of broth.

 Lemony Chargrilled Asparagus and Chicken Salad Toss 500 g (1 lb) trimmed asparagus spears in 1 tablespoon olive oil. Heat a ridged griddle pan over a high heat and griddle the asparagus for 4–5 minutes until tender and charred, turning frequently. Meanwhile, roughly slice 400 g (13 oz) poached or roasted chicken breast and toss with 250 g (8 oz) mixed baby leaf salad leaves. Arrange the chicken and leaves on serving plates and top with the asparagus. Drizzle over 4 tablespoons reduced-fat, lemony salad dressing and serve.

 Thai Red Curry Chicken and Vegetable Broth Cut 200 g (7 oz) baby courgettes and 200 g (7 oz) baby carrots into thin batons, slice 125 g (4 oz) trimmed fine asparagus tips lengthways and thinly shred 1 baby green cabbage. Heat 2 teaspoons vegetable oil in a wok over a medium heat, then add the vegetables and stir-fry for 3–4 minutes until beginning to soften. Add 2 tablespoons Thai red curry paste and stir-fry for 1 minute, then add 400 g (13 oz) can reduced-fat coconut milk, 400 ml (14 fl oz) hot chicken stock, 2 tablespoons fish sauce and 300 g (10 oz) sliced chicken breast and simmer gently for 4–5 minutes or until the chicken is cooked. Meanwhile, heat 375 g (12 oz) cooked rice noodles. Spoon the noodles into serving bowls, ladle over the broth and serve.

LOW-MEAT-WEP

30 Madeira and Rosemary Pork Medallions

Serves 4

25 g (1 oz) dry-packed sun-dried tomatoes

1.25 kg (2½ lb) large potatoes, peeled and quartered

2 tablespoons olive oil

750 g (1½ lb) pork fillet, cut into 1.5 cm (¾ inch) slices

3 shallots, finely sliced

50 ml (2 fl oz) Madeira

4 teaspoons finely chopped rosemary

125 ml (4 fl oz) low-fat single cream

1 tablespoon wholegrain mustard

75 ml (3 fl oz) skimmed milk

salt and pepper

- Place the sun-dried tomatoes in a bowl and cover with just-boiled water. Cover the bowl and set aside for 20 minutes.

- Put the potatoes in a large saucepan and cover with salted water. Bring to the boil and cook for 15–20 minutes.

- Heat the olive oil in a large frying pan over a medium-high heat, add the pork and cook for 1–2 minutes until golden, turning once. Remove from the pan and set aside.

- Reduce the heat to medium, add the shallots to the pan and cook for 4–5 minutes until softened and golden. Pour in the Madeira and add 2 teaspoons of the rosemary. Allow to bubble, then stir in the cream, season generously with salt and pepper and simmer for 1–2 minutes to heat through.

- Drain the soaked tomatoes, reserving 2 tablespoons of the soaking liquid, then slice into strips. Add the pork, tomatoes and reserved liquid to the pan. Simmer gently for 3–4 minutes.

- Meanwhile, drain the potatoes and mash with the mustard, remaining rosemary and milk. Season well with salt and pepper. Serve the mash with the pork medallions on top.

10 Smoked Bacon and Rosemary Pasta

Sauce Cut 4 slices of lean, smoked back bacon into strips and fry in 1 tablespoon olive oil until crispy. Add 3 finely chopped shallots, stir-fry for 2–3 minutes, then add 25 g (1 oz) thinly sliced drained sun-dried tomatoes in oil, 4 teaspoons finely chopped rosemary and 50 ml (2 fl oz) Madeira. Bubble up, add 125 ml (4 fl oz) low-fat single cream, season and simmer until hot. Serve with cooked fresh tagliatelle.

20 Pan-Fried Pork Loin with Rosemary and Cider Vinegar

Sauce Heat 2 teaspoons olive oil in a large frying pan over a medium heat, then add 4 lean pork loin steaks, about 150 g (5 oz) each, and fry for 1–2 minutes each side or until browned. Remove the steaks from the pan and set aside. Add 2 chopped slices of lean smoked bacon to the pan and stir-fry for 2–3 minutes, then add 3 finely chopped shallots and cook for

3–4 minutes, stirring occasionally. Add 4 teaspoons finely chopped rosemary, 125 ml (4 fl oz) dry cider and 50 ml (2 fl oz) cider vinegar and return the pork to the pan. Simmer gently for 3–4 minutes until the pork is cooked through, then stir in 100 ml (3½ fl oz) low-fat single cream and heat until the sauce is hot. Serve with steamed purple sprouting broccoli.

20 Turkey Breast with Prosciutto, Sage and Capers

Serves 4

4 turkey breast fillet steaks or escalopes, about 150 g (5 oz) each
8 lean slices prosciutto or Parma ham
8 sage leaves
2 tablespoons plain flour
light olive oil spray
500 g (1 lb) fresh tagliatelle
2 tablespoons Marsala
125ml (4 fl oz) dry white wine
1 tablespoon capers, rinsed and drained, or 8 caperberries
pepper

- Place a turkey escalope between 2 layers of clingfilm and beat with a rolling pin to flatten. Fold a slice of ham in half and place it over the turkey, then top the ham with 2 sage leaves, securing with cocktail sticks. Repeat with the other escalopes. Season the flour with pepper and sprinkle over the top.

- Place a large, nonstick frying pan over a medium-high heat, spray with a little oil and fry the turkey in batches, for 2–3 minutes on each side until golden brown.

- Meanwhile, bring a large saucepan of salted water to the boil and cook the tagliatelle for 3–4 minutes until 'al dente', or according to the packet instructions, then drain.

- Add the Marsala to the pan with the escalopes, followed by the white wine and capers, scraping the base gently with a wooden spatula to deglaze the pan. Turn the escalopes over and bubble gently for another 1–2 minutes

- Transfer the pasta to serving plates, place the escalopes on top and spoon over the juices to serve.

10 Chicken, Prosciutto and Sage Open Ciabatta Sandwich Split open 4 ciabatta rolls and griddle the cut sides on a ridged griddle pan over a medium-high heat. Top each ciabatta base with 50 g (2 oz) thickly sliced cooked chicken, a slice of prosciutto or Parma ham, 2 slices of beef tomato, 1 finely chopped sage leaf and ½ teaspoon rinsed and drained capers. Season with black pepper, top with a small handful of lamb's lettuce and serve as an open sandwich with the lid resting by the base.

30 Roasted Turkey, Prosciutto, Sage and Caperberry Rolls Prepare the turkey escalopes as above, layering them with the ham and sage leaves but without securing with cocktails sticks. Roughly chop 8 caperberries and scatter over the escalopes. Roll up each piece of turkey tightly, securing each with a cocktail stick. Arrange the rolls in a shallow, ovenproof dish and place in a preheated oven, 200°C (400°F), Gas Mark 6, for 10 minutes. Add 2 tablespoons marsala and 125ml (4 fl oz) dry white wine to the dish, then bake for a further 8–10 minutes until the turkey is cooked through. Remove and serve, cut in half diagonally, with 500 g (1 lb) cooked fresh tagliatelle.

30 Grilled Barbecue Pork Skewers with Crunchy Coleslaw

Serves 4

600 g (1 lb 3½ oz) lean pork loin, cut into cubes

1 tablespoon red wine vinegar

2 teaspoons piri-piri sauce

½ teaspoon granulated sugar

4–6 tablespoons extra-light mayonnaise

½ red cabbage, shredded

2 carrots, grated

2 spring onions, trimmed and thinly sliced

salt and pepper

Barbecue marinade

2 tablespoons muscovado sugar

2 tablespoons tomato ketchup

2 tablespoons dark soy sauce

1 teaspoon Chinese 5-spice powder

2 tablespoons freshly squeezed orange juice

- To make the barbecue marinade, mix together the sugar, tomato ketchup, soy sauce, Chinese 5-spice powder and orange juice in a large bowl until smooth. Tip the pork loin into the bowl and mix until the pork is well coated with the marinade. Set aside to marinate for 15 minutes.

- Combine the vinegar, piri-piri sauce, granulated sugar and mayonnaise in a small bowl to make the coleslaw dressing. Toss the cabbage, carrots and spring onions together in a large bowl, then add the dressing and mix until all the ingredients are well combined. Season with salt and pepper and set aside.

- Preheat the grill. Thread the marinated pork on to 8 metal skewers and place under the grill for 7–10 minutes, turning occasionally, until cooked through and sticky.

- Serve the pork skewers with the coleslaw and with sticky Thai rice, if liked.

 Spicy Barbecued Grilled Pork Steaks

Smother 6 thin, lean pork loin steaks, about 450 g (14½ oz) total weight, with 6 tablespoons ready-made spicy barbecue marinade. Place on a baking sheet grill for 7–8 minutes until cooked and sticky, turning once and brushing with extra marinade. When the pork is cooked, carefully cut into strips and serve with 450 g (14½ oz) ready-made, reduced-fat coleslaw. Sprinkle with a few dashes of piri-piri sauce to season.

 Braised Pork in an Orange Barbecue Sauce Make the barbecue marinade as above, adding an extra 75 ml (3 fl oz) freshly squeezed orange juice. Pour the marinade into a large saucepan over a low heat and warm gently to dissolve the sugar. Add 600 g (1 lb 2 oz) cubed lean pork loin and simmer gently for 10–12 minutes until just cooked through. Serve with steamed sticky Thai rice, steamed mangetout and scatter with 2 sliced spring onions.

QuickCook
Vegetarian

Recipes listed by cooking time

30

20

10

30 Quinoa-Stuffed Beef Tomatoes with Melting Mozzarella

Serves 4

400 ml (14 fl oz) vegetable stock

200 g (7 oz) quinoa, rinsed under running water

1 tablespoon extra virgin rapeseed oil

200 g (7 oz) chestnut mushrooms, chopped

2 small courgettes, diced

2 spring onions, finely chopped

2 tablespoons toasted sunflower seeds

1 small bunch of chopped basil

finely grated zest of 1 lemon

8 small or 4 large tomatoes

125 g (4 oz) reduced-fat mozzarella, sliced

salt and pepper

- Pour the vegetable stock into a medium-sized saucepan and bring to the boil. Tip the quinoa into the pan, cover and simmer gently for 12–15 minutes. It is ready when the seed begins to come away from the germ. Remove from the heat and drain off any stock that hasn't been absorbed.

- Meanwhile, preheat the oven to 200°C (400°F), Gas Mark 6 and heat the oil in a large frying pan over a medium heat. Add the mushrooms and cook, stirring, for 4–5 minutes, then add the courgettes. Cook for a further 4–5 minutes, then stir in the spring onions, sunflower seeds, basil, lemon rind and cooked quinoa and season well with salt and pepper.

- Cut the tops off the tomatoes and scoop out the seeds. Spoon the quinoa mixture into the tomatoes, then top each tomato with the sliced mozzarella. Place on a lightly greased baking tray. Replace the lids, then bake in the oven for 15–18 minutes until the mozzarella melts. Serve with crisp salad leaves.

 Mixed Vegetable Quinoa Cook the quinoa as above. Meanwhile, heat 1 tablespoon extra virgin rapeseed oil in a large frying pan over a medium heat. Add 200 g (7 oz) chopped chestnut mushrooms and fry for 4–5 minutes, stirring, then add 250 g (8 oz) defrosted frozen peas, 200 g (7 oz) can sweetcorn, drained, 2 chopped spring onions and 1 chopped small bunch of basil. Stir-fry until heated through, then remove from the heat, toss through the quinoa and scatter over 125 g (4 oz) diced mozzarella. Serve with lemon wedges and green salad.

 Grilled Mushroom and Couscous-Stuffed Tomatoes Heat 1 tablespoon extra virgin rapeseed oil in a large frying pan over a medium heat, then add 200 g (7 oz) chopped chestnut mushrooms and fry for 4–5 minutes, stirring occasionally. Meanwhile, pour 350 ml (12 fl oz) boiling water over 225 g (7½ oz) quick-cook roasted vegetable couscous and leave to stand for 5 minutes. Fluff the couscous with a fork, then mix through the cooked mushrooms, 2 tablespoons each of chopped parsley and mint, the grated rind of 1 lemon and 1 cored, deseeded and finely chopped green pepper. Cut the tops off 8 small or 4 large tomatoes, then stuff with the couscous mixture. Crumble 150 g (5 oz) reduced-fat feta over the tops, place the tomatoes on a grill rack and slide under a preheated grill for 5–6 minutes until hot and golden. Serve with lemon wedges and salad leaves.

Chilli-Spiked Broccoli with Linguine

Serves 4

400 g (13 oz) linguine
1½ tablespoons olive oil
2 garlic cloves, finely sliced
1 large red chilli, finely chopped
3 tablespoons lemon juice
200 ml (7 fl oz) vegetable stock
300 g (10 oz) purple sprouting
  broccoli stalks, cut into 2.5–
  3.5 cm (1–1½ inch) lengths,
  or broccoli florets
2–3 tablespoons pecorino cheese
  with black pepper or mature
  pecorino, finely grated (optional)
salt and pepper

- Bring a large pan of lightly salted water to the boil and cook the linguine for 11 minutes until 'al dente', or according to the packet instructions.

- Meanwhile, heat the olive oil in a small frying pan over a low heat, then add the garlic and chilli and cook gently for 3–4 minutes until tender. Stir in the lemon juice and vegetable stock and bring to the boil.

- Add the broccoli stalks or florets to the stock, then cover and simmer gently for 2–3 minutes until just 'al dente', turning occasionally. Season generously with salt and pepper.

- Toss the broccoli and chilli-spiked stock gently with the drained pasta, then heap into deep bowls and serve immediately sprinkled with the grated pecorino, if using.

 Chilli-Spiked Asparagus with Penne Cook 500 g (1 lb) fresh penne in salted boiling water for 4–5 minutes until 'al dente', or according to the packet instructions. Meanwhile, heat 1½ tablespoons olive oil in a small frying pan over a low heat, add 2 finely sliced garlic cloves and 1 finely chopped large red chilli and cook gently for 3–4 minutes. Stir in 3 tablespoons lemon juice and 100 ml (7 fl oz) vegetable stock and bring to the boil. Tip in 300 g (10 oz) trimmed asparagus tips, cover and simmer gently for 2–3 minutes until 'al dente', turning occasionally. Season generously with salt and pepper, then toss with the penne.

 Creamy Chilli-Spiked Baked Penne Cook 500 g (1 lb) fresh penne in lightly salted boiling water for 4–5 minutes until 'al dente', or according to the packet instructions, adding 300 g (10 oz) broccoli florets for the final 3 minutes of cooking. Meanwhile, heat 1½ tablespoons olive oil in a small frying pan over a low heat, then add 2 finely sliced garlic cloves and 1 large finely chopped red chilli and cook gently for 3–4 minutes until tender. Stir in 150 ml (¼ pint) hot vegetable stock and 125 ml (4 fl oz) reduced-fat single cream, then toss with the drained pasta and broccoli. Season generously with salt and pepper, then pour the pasta into a large, ovenproof dish and sprinkle with 2–3 tablespoons grated mature pecorino cheese. Put in a preheated oven, 200°C (400°F), Gas Mark 6, for 15–18 minutes until golden and bubbling.

30 Falafel Patties with Wholemeal Pitta

Serves 4

2 x 400 g (13 oz) cans chickpeas, drained
1 teaspoon ground cumin
1 teaspoon ground coriander
1 small red onion, finely grated
3 carrots, 1 finely grated, 2 coarsely grated
2 garlic cloves, finely chopped
4 tablespoons finely chopped parsley
1 egg, lightly beaten
1 teaspoon lemon rind
4 tablespoons plain flour
2 teaspoons baking powder
½ teaspoon chilli flakes (optional)
vegetable oil, for greasing
4 warmed wholemeal pitta breads
200 g (7 oz) low-fat tzatziki
salt and pepper

- Preheat the oven to 200°C (400°F), Gas Mark 6. Place the chickpeas, cumin and coriander in a food processor or blender and pulse until the chickpeas resemble coarse breadcrumbs. Scrape into a large bowl and add the onion, finely grated carrot, garlic, parsley, egg, lemon rind, flour, baking powder and chilli flakes and mix until well combined.

- Lightly grease a nonstick baking sheet and form walnut-sized spoonfuls of the mixture into 24 slightly flattened patties and place on the baking sheet. Put the falafel in the oven and for 12–15 minutes until golden and crisp.

- Arrange the patties inside warmed wholemeal pittas and serve with the grated carrots and low-fat tzatziki.

1 Chickpea Salad

Rinse and drain 2 x 400 g (13 oz) cans chickpeas and place in a large bowl with 1 finely chopped red onion, 2 coarsely grated carrots, 4 tablespoons finely chopped parsley, 2 tablespoons chopped mint, the grated rind and juice of 1 lemon and ½ teaspoon chilli flakes. Season generously with salt and pepper and stir to combine. Spoon on to serving plates and drizzle 1 teaspoon olive oil over each salad. Serve with warmed wholemeal pitta breads and tzatziki.

2 Falafel Burgers

Make the falafel mixture as above. Form into 8 large burgers and heat 1 tablespoon olive oil in a large, nonstick frying pan over a medium heat. Cook for 7–8 minutes until crisp and golden, turning once. Drain the burgers on kitchen paper to remove any excess oil, then arrange inside warmed wholemeal burger buns with tzatziki, crispy iceberg lettuce and sliced tomato.

 # Watermelon, Pomegranate and Haloumi Salad

Serves 4

200 g (7 oz) reduced-fat haloumi cheese, cut into 8 slices

finely grated zest and juice of 1 lime

2 spring onions, finely sliced

2 tablespoons chopped parsley

2 tablespoons chopped mint

1 tablespoon avocado oil

150 g (5 oz) wild rocket leaves

½ watermelon, peeled, deseeded and diced

½ small red onion, finely sliced

100 g (3½ oz) almond-stuffed green olives

1 tablespoon pomegranate molasses

1–2 teaspoons chilli paste, to taste

100 g (3½ oz) pomegranate seeds (about 1 pomegranate)

pepper

- Preheat the grill. Toss the haloumi with the lime zest, spring onions and 1 tablespoon each of the parsley and mint, then place on a foil-lined baking tray. Drizzle over a little of the avocado oil and place the tray under the grill for 3–4 minutes until hot and golden, turning once.

- Meanwhile, arrange the rocket leaves on 4 large plates. Toss the watermelon, onion, olives and remaining parsley and mint in a large bowl. Spoon the dressed watermelon over the rocket.

- In a small bowl, mix together the lime juice, pomegranate molasses, the remaining avocado oil and chilli paste, to taste, then season with black pepper.

- Top each salad with 2 slices of the grilled haloumi, then scatter over the pomegranate seeds. Serve drizzled with the dressing.

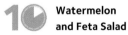

Watermelon and Feta Salad

Peel, deseed and dice ½ watermelon and arrange on serving plates. Crumble 200 g (7 oz) reduced-fat feta over the watermelon, then scatter 2 finely sliced spring onions, 2 tablespoon each of chopped mint and parsley and 100 g (3½ oz) black olives. Sprinkle over 100 g (3½ oz) pomegranate seeds and serve drizzled with 1 tablespoon pomegranate molasses.

Sweet Potato and Haloumi Salad with a Herb Dressing

Cook 500 g (1 lb) peeled sweet potatoes cut into 1.5 cm (¾ inch) slices in boiling water for 4–5 minutes to partially cook. Meanwhile, rub 1 teaspoon avocado oil over 200 g (7 oz) reduced-fat haloumi cheese, cut into 8 slices. Heat a ridged griddle pan over a medium heat, then griddle the haloumi for 3–4 minutes, turning once. Remove and set aside. Brush the parboiled sweet potato with 1 tablespoon chilli oil on both sides, then griddle for 2–3 minutes each side, turning the pieces once to create a criss-cross pattern. Meanwhile, arrange 150 g (5 oz) wild rocket leaves on serving plates and mix together in a small bowl 1 tablespoon each of reduced-fat pesto and lemon juice. Arrange the sweet potato and haloumi on the rocket leaves, then scatter over 2 finely sliced spring onions and 2 tablespoons each of chopped parsley and mint. Drizzle over the lemon dressing and serve scattered with 1 tablespoon toasted pine nuts.

30 One-Pot Southern-Style Rice

Serves 4

1½ tablespoons vegetable oil
1 large onion, chopped
2 garlic cloves, roughly chopped
1 celery stick, chopped
1 red and 1 yellow pepper, chopped
1 courgette, chopped
1 teaspoon each dried thyme, dried
   oregano, hot smoked paprika
¼ teaspoon cayenne pepper
250 g (8 oz) long-grain rice,
   rinsed under running cold water
2 tablespoons tomato purée
2 x 400 g (13 oz) cans chopped
   tomatoes
450 ml (¾ pint) vegetable stock
salt and pepper
2 tablespoons chopped parsley
few dashes Tabasco sauce

- Heat the oil in a large, heavy-based casserole over a medium heat. Add the onion, garlic, celery and red and yellow peppers and cook for 4–5 minutes, stirring frequently, then add the courgette and cook for a further 3–4 minutes.

- Add the herbs, spices and rice and stir-fry for 1 minute, coating the rice well in the other ingredients. Stir in the tomato purée, chopped tomatoes and vegetable stock and season with salt and pepper. Bring to the boil and cover with a tight fitting lid, then reduce the heat and leave to simmer gently for 15–18 minutes until the rice is cooked and the mixture thickened.

- Serve sprinkled with chopped parsley and a few dashes of Tabasco sauce, if liked.

 5 Mixed-Bean and Rice Salad

Mix together a 400 g (13 oz) can 5 mixed-beans, drained, a 200 g (7 oz) can sweetcorn, drained, and 250 g (8 oz) cold, steamed rice. Finely chop, 1 red pepper, 1 yellow pepper, 1 stick of celery, 2 spring onions and 200 g (7 oz) quartered cherry tomatoes. Add 3 tablespoons lime juice, 2 teaspoons Tabasco sauce, 1 tablespoon vegetable oil and 1 chopped small bunch of flat-leaf parsley and toss. Serve in bowls, topped with reduced-fat soured cream and toasted flour tortillas.

 Southern-Style Mixed Vegetable and Bean Stir-Fry Chop 1 large onion, 1 celery stick and 1 courgette. Deseed and chop 1 red and 1 yellow pepper and finely chop 2 garlic cloves. Roughly chop 2 tablespoons pickled red jalapeño peppers and set aside. Heat 1½ tablespoons vegetable oil in a large frying pan or wok over a medium heat, then add the raw vegetables and stir-fry for 10 minutes until tender. Add 1 teaspoon each of dried thyme, dried oregano and hot smoked paprika and

¼ teaspoon cayenne pepper and stir-fry for a further minute. Stir in 250 g (8 oz) steamed plain, mushroom or chilli and bean rice, then add a 400 g (13 oz) can kidney beans, drained. Continue to stir-fry until hot, then serve immediately in bowls, each topped with a dollop of reduced-fat soured cream and a scattering of chopped pickled red jalapeño peppers.

1 Green Lentil Tapenade with Toast

Serves 4

250 g (8 oz) ready-to-eat green Puy lentils, rinsed and drained
2 tablespoons black olive paste
1 tablespoon caper paste or capers, rinsed, drained and finely chopped
1 tablespoon lemon juice
50 g (2 oz) ready-to-eat slow-roasted tomatoes (not in oil)
2 tablespoons toasted pine nuts
½ teaspoon hot smoked paprika
salt and pepper
hot toast, to serve

- Place all of the ingredients in a food processor or blender and pulse to blend until smooth.

- Scrape into a bowl and serve spread over hot toast.

2 Warm Puy Lentil Salad

Heat 1 tablespoon olive oil in a frying pan over a medium heat, add 3 finely chopped spring onions and 2 finely chopped garlic cloves and cook gently for 6–7 minutes, stirring. Add 1 tablespoon finely chopped capers, 50 g (2 oz) chopped ready-to-eat slow-roasted tomatoes (not in oil), ½ teaspoon hot smoked paprika and 500 g (1 lb) ready-to-eat cooked Puy lentils and stir to heat through. Meanwhile, mix 2 tablespoons each of lemon and black olive paste in a small bowl, then stir into the warm salad with 3 tablespoons chopped flat leaf parsley and salt and pepper, to taste. Serve in bowls with wild rocket leaves and hot toast.

3 Lentil and Spiced Tomato Casserole

Gently heat 1 tablespoon vegetable oil in a large casserole dish over a medium-low heat. Add 1 chopped onion and 2 finely sliced garlic cloves and cook for 7–8 minutes until softened, then add ½ teaspoon hot smoked paprika, 1 teaspoon each of ground coriander and cumin seeds, stirring until the onion is well coated in the spices. Tip in 150 g (5 oz) Puy lentils and 50 g (2 oz) roughly chopped ready-to-eat slow-roasted tomatoes (not in oil) and stir-fry for 1–2 minutes, then add 2 tablespoons each of tomato purée and black olive paste and 750 ml (1¼ pint) of hot vegetable stock. Season generously with salt and pepper, then gently simmer for about 18 minutes or until the lentils are tender. Scatter over 1 tablespoon rinsed and drained capers and serve with hot toast.

# Wholewheat Penne in a Tomato, Artichoke and Olive Sauce

Serves 4

1 tablespoon olive oil

1 onion, finely chopped

2 garlic cloves, finely chopped

50 ml (2 fl oz) red wine

2 x 400 g (13 oz) cans chopped tomatoes

pinch of sugar

1 teaspoon finely grated lemon rind

1 teaspoon dried oregano

75 g (3 oz) dry pitted black olives, roughly chopped

400 g (13 oz) wholewheat penne

1 small bunch of basil, leaves torn

400 g (13 oz) can artichokes, rinsed, drained and roughly chopped

salt and pepper

- Heat the olive oil in a large, heavy-based pan over a medium-low heat, then add the onion and garlic and cook gently for 5–6 minutes until softened. Stir in the red wine, tomatoes, sugar, lemon rind, oregano and black olives and bring to the boil. Reduce the heat and simmer gently for 12–15 minutes.

- Meanwhile, bring a large saucepan of lightly salted water to the boil and cook the pasta for 11 minutes until 'al dente', or according to the packet instructions.

- Add the basil and artichokes to the pasta sauce and stir until the artichokes are heated through. Season with salt and pepper.

- Drain the pasta and serve in large bowls with the pasta sauce spooned over. Serve accompanied with a green salad.

Tomato and Artichoke Bruschetta

Roughly chop 3 tomatoes and place in a bowl with 1 teaspoon dried oregano, 75 g (3 oz) roughly chopped dry pitted black olives, 400 g (13 oz) can artichokes, rinsed, drained and chopped, 1 sliced spring onion, 1 tablespoon lemon juice and 1 tablespoon olive oil. Stir gently, then season with salt and pepper. Toast 4 large slices sourdough bread and rub the surface with the cut edges of 1 garlic clove. Place on serving plates, spoon over the tomato topping and scatter with basil leaves.

Artichoke and Broccoli Bake

Heat 1 tablespoon olive oil in a large saucepan and fry 2 finely chopped garlic cloves over a medium heat for 1 minute. Add 50 ml (2 fl oz) red wine, 2 x 400 g (13 oz) cans chopped tomatoes, a pinch of sugar, 1 teaspoon finely grated lemon rind, 1 teaspoon dried oregano and 75 g (3 oz) roughly chopped dry pitted black olives. Bring to the boil, then reduce the heat and simmer gently for 7–8 minutes. Meanwhile, cook 500 g (1 lb) fresh penne pasta in a large

saucepan of lightly salted boiling water with 200 g (7 oz) small broccoli florets for 3–4 minutes until the pasta is 'al dente', or according to the packet instructions. Drain the pasta and broccoli, then stir into the tomato sauce. Add 400 g (13 oz) can artichokes, rinsed, drained and roughly chopped, then scrape the mixture into an ovenproof dish. Top with 125 g (4 oz) ricotta in small spoonfuls and bake in a preheated oven, 220°C (425°F), Gas Mark 7, for about 18 minutes or until hot and bubbling.

30 Red Quinoa, Lemon and Tomato Salad with Feta

Serves 4

150 g (5 oz) red quinoa, rinsed under running cold water
300 ml (½ pint) boiling water
4 yellow or red tomatoes, deseeded and diced
1 large green pepper, finely chopped
2 spring onions, finely sliced
100 g (3½ oz) pitted Kalamata olives, roughly chopped
½ cucumber, cut in half lengthways, deseeded and sliced
grated rind and juice of 1 lemon
3 tablespoons chopped parsley
3 tablespoons chopped mint
4 small red or white chicory, sliced
100 g (3½ oz) reduced-fat feta
2 tablespoons toasted mixed seeds
small handful of alfalfa sprouts

- Tip the quinoa into a medium-sized saucepan and pour over the measured boiling water. Cover the pan and simmer gently for about 12–15 minutes. It is ready when the seed begins to come away from the germ. Drain the quinoa into a fine sieve and cool under running cold water. Drain well.

- Meanwhile, mix together in a large bowl the tomatoes, pepper, spring onions, olives and cucumber, then stir in the lemon rind, parsley and mint.

- Mix the cooled quinoa through the vegetables and season with salt, pepper and lemon juice, to taste. Set aside for 5–10 minutes to allow the flavours to develop.

- Scatter the chicory on to 4 serving plates, spoon over the quinoa salad and crumble over the feta. Sprinkle with the toasted seeds and alfalfa sprouts and serve.

 Minted Pea Quinoa Heat 250 g (8 oz) ready-to-eat red and white quinoa or ready-to-eat red mixed wholesome grains, according to the packet instructions. Tip the quinoa or grains into a bowl and toss with 3 tablespoons each of chopped parsley and mint, 125 g (4 oz) thawed peas and 2 finely sliced spring onions. Season with salt, pepper and lemon juice, to taste, and crumble over 100 g (3½ oz) Wensleydale cheese or a similar crumbly white cheese. Sprinkle over 2 tablespoons toasted mixed seeds and serve.

 Spicy Pepper and Onion Quinoa Rinse 150 g (5 oz) red quinoa under running water, then cook gently in twice its volume of boiling water for 12–15 minutes until tender. It is done when the seed begins to come away from the germ. Tip the quinoa into a fine sieve and drain away any excess water. Meanwhile, mix together the juice of 1 lemon, 1 tablespoon each of olive oil and mild harissa and 3 tablespoons each of chopped parsley and mint. Set aside. Heat 1 tablespoon olive oil in a frying pan over a medium heat. Add 1 chopped red onion, 1 deseeded and finely chopped green pepper and 2 chopped garlic cloves and cook for 5–6 minutes, stirring occasionally, then stir in 1 teaspoon cumin seeds. When the quinoa is ready, fork through the lemon dressing, fold in the vegetables and serve.

30 More Than 5 Vegetable Pizza

Serves 4

250 g (8 oz) peeled and diced sweet potato
6 tablespoons thick Italian passata
2 tablespoons chopped basil
pinch of sugar
1 teaspoon dried thyme
300 g (10 oz) packet pizza mix
plain flour, for dusting
150 g (5 oz) mushrooms, thinly sliced
1 small red pepper, thinly sliced
½ red onion, thinly sliced
75 g (3 oz) frozen petit pois
75 g (3 oz) baby leaf spinach, shredded
1 tablespoon pine nuts
1–2 tablespoons finely grated Parmesan cheese (optional)
salt and pepper

- Place the sweet potato in a pan of lightly salted boiling water and cook for 10–12 minutes until tender.

- Meanwhile, preheat the oven to 220°C (425°F), Gas Mark 7, and in a small bowl mix together the passata, basil and sugar, then season with salt and pepper.

- Drain the sweet potato, then return to the pan and mash with the dried thyme. Scrape into a large bowl and stir in the packet pizza mix. Add enough warm water, about 4–6 tablespoons, to make a dough. Tip the dough out onto a lightly floured surface and knead briefly until smooth, then roll out to fit a large nonstick baking sheet.

- Spread the passata mixture over the surface of the dough, leaving a border of 1 cm (½ inch). Top with the mushrooms, red pepper and onion, then scatter over the peas, spinach and pine nuts. Sprinkle over the Parmesan, if using.

- Put the pizza in the oven for 12–14 minutes until crisp and golden. Serve with rocket and spinach salad leaves.

10 Mushroom, Pepper and Onion Baguette

Subs Cut a long baguette in half and then cut in half lengthways to create 4 subs. Grill, cut side up, for 1 minute. Mix 6 tablespoons thick passata, 2 tablespoons chopped basil and a pinch of sugar. Spread over each baguette. Scatter over sliced mushrooms, red pepper and ½ red onion as above, then sprinkle over 2 tablespoons grated Parmesan cheese. Grill for 5–6 minutes until crisp. Scatter over 75 g (3 oz) baby leaf spinach and 1 tablespoon pine nuts and serve.

20 Mushroom, Pepper and Onion Calzone

Thinly slice 150 g (5 oz) mushrooms and ½ red onion, deseed and thinly slice 1 small red pepper and roughly chop basil leaves to give 2 tablespoons. Pour a 300 g (10 oz) packet of pizza mix into a large bowl, then add enough water to make a soft dough, following the packet instructions. Tip the dough on to a lightly floured surface and knead into a ball, then cut in half and roll into 2 large circles. Top half of each pizza base with the mushrooms, onion, pepper, basil and ½ teaspoon dried thyme. Fold the uncovered dough over the vegetables and pinch down the edges to seal. Place in a preheated oven, 220°C (425°F), Gas Mark 7, for 10–12 minutes until puffed up and golden. Meanwhile, heat 6 tablespoons thick Italian passata. Remove the calzone from the oven, cut in half, pour over the warmed passata and serve half per person. Scatter with rocket salad before serving.

LOW-FAST-GEV

10 Marinated Tofu with Sesame Seeds

Serves 4

320 g (11 oz) marinated tofu cubes

2 teaspoons toasted sesame seed oil

500 g (1 lb) mixed stir-fry vegetables

50 ml (2 fl oz) rice wine or dry sherry

2 tablespoons tamari or dark soy sauce

50 ml (2 fl oz) mirin

1 garlic clove, finely chopped

1 teaspoon grated fresh root ginger

1 tablespoon palm sugar or soft light brown sugar

1 tablespoon toasted sesame seeds

steamed Thai rice, to serve

- Pat the tofu with kitchen paper to remove excess oil.

- Heat the oil in wok over a medium heat, then add the mixed stir-fry vegetables and stir-fry for 2–3 minutes until starting to wilt.

- Add the tofu, rice wine, tamari or dark soy sauce, mirin, garlic, ginger and sugar and simmer for 1–2 minutes, stirring frequently. Scatter over the sesame seeds, then serve immediately with steamed Thai rice.

 20 Marinated Tofu Salad

Cut 2 carrots, 10 radishes and ½ deseeded cucumber into matchsticks and pat 320 g (11 oz) marinated tofu cubes with kitchen paper to remove excess oil. Tip the vegetable matchsticks and tofu into a bowl, then add 150 g (5 oz) bean sprouts and toss. In a separate bowl mix 1 teaspoon freshly grated ginger, 2 tablespoons lime juice, 1 teaspoon finely grated lime rind, 1 tablespoon vegetable oil, 2 tablespoons light soy sauce and 1 teaspoon palm sugar. Drizzle the dressing over and serve.

 30 Spicy Noodle Soup with Tofu

Pour 1.2 litres (2 pints) vegetable stock into a saucepan and place over a medium-high heat. Stir in 75 ml (3 fl oz) rice wine vinegar, 3 tablespoons dark soy sauce, 1 teaspoon freshly grated ginger, 1 finely chopped garlic clove, 1 tablespoon palm sugar or soft light brown sugar and 1 thinly sliced red chilli. Bring to the boil, then reduce the heat and simmer gently for 18–20 minutes until fragrant. Meanwhile, cook 250 g (8 oz) udon noodles in a large saucepan

of boiling water for 8–10 minutes until tender, or according to the packet instructions. Drain the noodles and spoon into serving bowls. Scatter 320 g (11 oz) marinated tofu cubes over the noodles and ladle over the soup. Serve immediately, garnished with 2 thinly sliced spring onions.

LOW–FAST–WYB

 # Lemon, Ricotta and Courgette Ribbons

Serves 4

400 g (13 oz) small yellow and green baby courgettes

250 g (8 oz) parpardelle or tagliatelle

Lemony ricotta

1 teaspoon fennel seeds

¼ teaspoon chilli flakes (optional)

12–15 black peppercorns

250 g (8 oz) ricotta

¼ teaspoon freshly ground nutmeg

finely grated rind and juice of 1 lemon

- Bring a large saucepan of lightly salted water to the boil.

- Meanwhile, make the lemony ricotta by lightly crushing the fennel seeds with the chilli flakes, if using, and black peppercorns, then tip into a medium-sized bowl. Add the ricotta, nutmeg and lemon rind and juice, mixing well, then set aside.

- Slice the courgettes thinly into ribbons using a mandolin or sharp vegetable peeler.

- Tip the pasta into the pan of boiling water and cook for 6–7 minutes until 'al dente', or according to the packet instructions. Two minutes before the end of cooking, add the courgettes to soften.

- Drain the pasta and courgettes, reserving 2–3 tablespoons of the cooking liquid. Return the pasta, courgettes and reserved water to the pan, scrape in the lemony ricotta and stir gently to combine. Season with salt and pepper, then serve immediately with a green salad.

Crunchy Topped Lemony Ricotta and Courgette Bake

Make the pasta dish as above, omitting the fennel seeds from the lemony ricotta. Tip the pasta into a rectangular baking dish and sprinkle with 100 g (3½ oz) freshly made, wholemeal breadcrumbs and 1 teaspoon fennel seeds. Place under a hot grill for 2–3 minutes until the breadcrumbs are golden brown and the fennel seeds fragrant. Remove and serve immediately.

 Lemony Ricotta Tagliatelle

Make the lemony ricotta, as above. Cook 500 g (1 lb) fresh tagliatelle in lightly salted boiling water for 6–7 minutes until 'al dente', or according to the packet instruction. While the pasta is cooking, coarsely grate 400 g (13 oz) small yellow and green baby courgettes. Drain the pasta and return to the pan over a medium heat. Add the grated courgette and lemony ricotta and stir to heat through. Serve immediately with a green salad.

30 Moroccan-Style Potato Bake

Serves 4

750 g (1½ lb) baby new potatoes, cut in half

1 litre (1¾ pints) hot vegetable stock

1 tablespoon olive oil

1 large red onion, halved and thinly sliced

2 garlic cloves, chopped

1 preserved lemon, finely chopped

250 g (8 oz) drained roasted peppers, sliced

1 teaspoon hot smoked paprika

1 teaspoon ground cumin

½ teaspoon ground ginger

2 tablespoons tomato purée

1 tablespoon aged sherry vinegar

salt and pepper

- Put the potatoes and vegetable stock in a large saucepan. Bring to the boil and cook, covered, for 12 minutes until tender but firm.

- Meanwhile, preheat the oven to 230°C (450°F), Gas Mark 8 and heat the olive oil in a large, deep-sided, ovenproof frying pan over a medium-low heat. Add the onion and fry gently for 3–4 minutes, then add the garlic and cook for a further 3–4 minutes until softened and lightly coloured.

- Stir into the onion mix the preserved lemon, roasted peppers, the spices, tomato purée, sherry vinegar and a little salt and pepper. Cook gently for 2 minutes.

- Drain the cooked potatoes, reserving 400 ml (14 fl oz) of the liquid, then add the potatoes and reserved stock to the pan. Bring up to the boil, then put the pan in oven and bake for 14–16 minutes until golden. Remove from the oven and serve immediately with a crisp green salad.

 Pan-Fried Moroccan-Style Vegetables Roughly chop 500 g (1 lb) cooked new potatoes and add to a large frying pan with 1 tablespoon olive oil, 1 teaspoon each of hot smoked paprika and ground cumin, ½ teaspoon ground ginger, 2 tablespoons tomato purée, 1 tablespoon aged sherry vinegar, 250 g (8 oz) drained roasted peppers, sliced, and 1 finely chopped preserved lemon. Stir to heat through, then serve over crisp green salad leaves with an extra drizzle of sherry vinegar.

 Moroccan-Style Chickpeas Cook 1 halved and thinly sliced large red onion and 2 chopped garlic cloves, as above, then add 1 teaspoon each of hot smoked paprika and ground cumin, ½ teaspoon ground ginger, 2 tablespoons tomato purée, 1 tablespoon aged sherry vinegar, 250 g (8 oz) drained roasted peppers, sliced, and 1 finely chopped preserved lemon. Season with salt and pepper and cook for 1–2 minutes, then stir in 2 x 400 g (13 oz) cans of rinsed and drained chickpeas and cook for 3–4 minutes, stirring occasionally. Fold in 125 g (4 oz) washed, trimmed and roughly chopped spinach, then sprinkle over an extra 1–2 tablespoons sherry vinegar, to taste. Cook for a further 1–2 minutes until the spinach has wilted. Serve immediately.

 # Vietnamese-Style Vegetable Noodle Salad

Serves 4

200 g (7 oz) vermicelli rice sticks
½ cucumber, deseeded and cut into matchsticks
1 carrot, cut into matchsticks
150 g (5 oz) bean sprouts
125 g mangetout, cut into thin strips
2 tablespoons chopped coriander
2 tablespoons chopped mint
1 red chilli, deseeded and finely sliced
2 tablespoons chopped blanched peanuts, to garnish

Dressing

1 tablespoon sunflower or groundnut oil
½ teaspoon caster sugar
1 tablespoon fish sauce
2 tablespoons freshly squeezed lime juice

- Bring a large saucepan of water to the boil, then turn off the heat and add the rice sticks. Cover and leave to cook for 4 minutes until just tender, or according to the packet instructions. Drain the noodles and cool immediately in a bowl of ice-cold water.

- To make the dressing, put the oil, caster sugar, fish sauce and lime juice in a small bowl and stir until the sugar is dissolved.

- Drain the noodles and return to the bowl. Pour over half of the dressing, then tip in the vegetables, herbs and chilli. Toss until well combined.

- Heap the noodle salad on serving plates and drizzle with the remaining dressing. Serve scattered with chopped peanuts.

 Quick Tofu and Bean Sprout Noodle Salad Make the dressing, as above. Toss 375 g (12 oz) precooked rice sticks with the dressing, 150 g (5 oz) bean sprouts, 300 g (10 oz) marinated tofu strips, 1 finely chopped red chilli and 2 tablespoons each of chopped coriander and mint. Serve in deep bowls with lime wedges on the side.

 Vegetable, Egg and Noodle Stir-Fry Cook 200 g (7 oz) vermicelli rice sticks and make the dressing as above, then toss half of the dressing through the noodles. In a small bowl beat together 2 eggs, 1 tablespoon soy sauce and 2 sliced spring onions. Heat 1 teaspoon groundnut oil in a wok over a medium-high heat, then pour in half the egg mixture. Swirl the wok to coat with the egg mixture and cook until crisp. Slide on to a plate, then repeat to make a second omelette. Roll up the omelettes tightly and cut into thin shreds. Heat a further teaspoon of oil in the wok, then stir-fry 2 finely sliced garlic cloves and 1 tablespoon chopped fresh root ginger for 30 seconds. Add 200 g (7 oz) sprouting broccoli stems and 150 g (5 oz) thinly sliced runner beans and stir-fry for 3–4 minutes until the vegetables are tender. Serve with the noodles, topped with the sliced omelette.

30 Meaty Mushrooms in Red Wine

Serves 4

2 garlic cloves, peeled
1 tablespoon olive oil
12 baby onions, cut in half
1 celery stick, roughly chopped
1 carrot, diced
300 g (10 oz) portobello or large flat mushrooms, thickly sliced
200 g (7 oz) button mushrooms
2 tablespoons good brandy
15 g ($\frac{1}{2}$ oz) butter
15 g ($\frac{1}{2}$ oz) plain flour
300 ml ($\frac{1}{2}$ pint) red wine
$\frac{1}{2}$ teaspoon soft dark brown sugar
2 tablespoons chopped parsley, to garnish
salt and pepper

- Cut the garlic in half then crush with the flat side of a knife to keep whole. Heat the oil in a large, heavy-based casserole over a medium-low heat. Add the garlic, onions, celery and carrot to the pan and cook gently for 8–10 minutes until golden.

- Add the mushrooms and cook for a further 5–7 minutes until the mushrooms are soft. Remove all the vegetables from the pan with a slotted spoon and set aside.

- Remove the pan from the heat, pour the brandy into the pan and carefully ignite, allowing all the alcohol to burn off. Place the pan over a low heat, then add the butter and flour and stir with a wooden spoon for 1–2 minutes. Slowly pour the red wine into the pan, stirring constantly until all incorporated. Add the sugar and continue stirring until the sauce thickens.

- Return the vegetables to the pan and simmer gently to reheat. Season generously with salt and pepper, sprinkle with chopped parsley and serve with mashed potatoes.

10 Garlic Mushroom Open Sandwich

Heat 1 tablespoon olive oil and 15 g ($\frac{1}{2}$ oz) butter in a large frying pan over a medium-low heat, add 2 finely chopped garlic cloves and fry gently for 1 minute. Add 300 g (10 oz) thickly sliced portobello or large flat field mushrooms to the pan and cook for 4–5 minutes until softened. Stir in 125 ml (4 fl oz) white wine and bubble for 2–3 minutes to evaporate. Stir in 2 tablespoons chopped parsley and serve on griddled or toasted bread.

20 Baked Whole Mushrooms on Griddled Bread Place 4 portobello or large flat field mushrooms on a nonstick baking tray. Scatter 2 finely chopped garlic cloves over the mushrooms and season with salt and pepper. Splash a little Cognac on to each mushroom and drizzle over 1 tablespoon olive oil. Put the mushrooms in a preheated oven, 200°C (400°F), Gas Mark 6, for 12–15 minutes or until tender. Divide 150 g (5 oz) watercress leaves among 4 serving plates, then place a

slice of griddled or toasted bread on each heap. Finish each stack with the baked mushrooms and serve immediately.

Quick Broad Bean, Pea and Fennel Salad with Sorrel

Serves 4

200 g (7 oz) frozen baby broad beans

150 g (5 oz) frozen petit pois

1 large fennel bulb, very thinly sliced

1 teaspoon lemon juice

100 g (3½ oz) sorrel leaves, washed and dried

4 sprigs mint, leaves removed and finely shredded

2–3 teaspoons avocado oil (optional)

salt and pepper

lemon wedges, to serve

- Bring a large saucepan of lightly salted water to the boil. Add the broad beans and simmer rapidly for 3 minutes, then add the peas. Bring back to the boil, then drain immediately and tip the broad beans and peas into a bowl of ice-cold water.

- Meanwhile, toss the fennel with the lemon juice and season with black pepper.

- Arrange the sorrel leaves in a large serving dish, then pile the fennel on the leaves, scatter over the peas and broad beans and sprinkle with shredded mint leaves.

- Drizzle over the avocado oil, if using, then season with a little salt and plenty of black pepper. Serve immediately with lemon wedges.

Chilled Fennel, Broad Bean and Pea Soup Bring a large saucepan of water to the boil, then add 1 chopped fennel bulb and cook for 5–6 minutes. Add 200 g (7 oz) frozen baby broad beans and simmer rapidly for a further 3 minutes, then add 150 g (5 oz) frozen petit pois. Bring back to the boil and cook for a further 1 minute, then drain into a colander and cool rapidly under cold running water. Drain well and then add to 400 ml (14 fl oz) cold vegetable stock. Place in a blender and blitz until silky smooth and season with salt and pepper. Serve in bowls with a dollop of half-fat crème fraîche on top and garnished with mint leaves.

Warm Potato Salad with Fennel, Broad Beans and Peas Cut 200 g (7 oz) baby new potatoes in half, then cook in a saucepan of lightly salted boiling water for 10–15 minutes until tender but firm. Meanwhile, arrange 1 thinly sliced fennel bulk in a single layer on a baking tray. Spray with a little olive oil and place in a preheated oven, 200°C (400°F), Gas Mark 6, for 15–20 minutes or until beginning to soften. Bring a large saucepan of lightly salted water to the boil. Add 200 g (7 oz) frozen baby broad beans and 150 g (5 oz) frozen petit pois and simmer rapidly for 3 minutes, then drain. Toss the warm potatoes, fennel, broad beans and peas with 100 g (3½ oz) washed and dried sorrel leaves, scatter with the chopped leaves from 4 sprigs of mint and serve immediately, drizzled with a little avocado oil, if liked.

30 Bean Burger with Chive and Onion Yogurt

Serves 4

400 g (13 oz) can black beans
400 g (13 oz) can adzuki beans
1 teaspoon celery salt
2 tablespoons sun-dried tomato
  paste or purée
2 teaspoons dried onion granules
1 teaspoon garlic powder
1 teaspoon ground cumin
4 tablespoons chopped coriander
1 egg, lightly beaten
100 g (3½ oz) fresh breadcrumbs
pinch of black pepper
2–3 tablespoons fine polenta or
  semolina, to dust
vegetable oil, for greasing
1 teaspoon cumin seeds
4 large plain or chilli and jalapeño
  soft tortilla wraps, to serve

Chive and onion yogurt

250 g (8 oz) fat-free Greek yogurt
½ small red onion, finely chopped
2 tablespoons chopped chives
1 tablespoon lime juice

- Preheat the oven to 220°C (425°F), Gas Mark 7. Drain the beans and place in a food processor with the celery salt, tomato paste, onion granules, parlic powder, ground cumin, coriander, egg, breadcrumbs and pepper and pulse until the mixture is combined but not smooth. Shape into 8 burgers and dust lightly with the polenta or semolina. Place on a lightly greased baking sheet and bake in the oven for 10–12 minutes, turning once, until cooked and crispy.

- Meanwhile, to make the chive and onion yogurt, mix together the yogurt, onion, chives and lime juice and season with salt and pepper. Cover with clingfilm and set aside in the fridge.

- Heat a small frying pan over medium heat and dry-roast the cumin seeds, stirring, until fragrant, then set aside to cool.

- Heat a ridged griddle pan over a medium-high heat and toast one side of a tortillas until lightly charred but not brittle. Fold into quarters, set aside and then repeat with the remaining tortillas. Scatter the cumin seeds over the chive and onion yogurt.

- When ready to serve, place 2 burgers inside each folded tortilla. Spoon in some chive and onion yogurt and serve with any remaining yogurt in a bowl on the side.

---

10 Black Bean Pâté

Put a 400 g (13 oz) can black beans, drained, in a food processor with 150 g (5 oz) can drained chickpeas, 4 tablespoons chopped coriander, 1 tablespoon lime juice, 2 teaspoons dried onion, 1 teaspoon each of celery salt, garlic powder and ground cumin. Pulse the mixture to a smooth-textured pâté, then season with salt and pepper. Serve spread on hot toast.

20 Chilli Bean Wraps

Mix together in a large bowl 400 g (13 oz) can black beans, drained, 400 g (13 oz) can adzuki beans, drained, 1 deseeded and finely chopped red pepper, 4 tablespoons finely chopped coriander, 2 tablespoons sun-dried tomato paste, 2 teaspoons dried onion and 1 teaspoon each of celery salt, garlic powder and ground cumin.

Spoon the mixture on 4 plain or chilli and jalapeño soft tortilla wraps, then roll up firmly and place in a snug-fitting ovenproof dish. Pour over 300 g (10 oz) spicy tomato salsa, then place in a preheated oven, 220°C (425°F), Gas Mark 7, for 15 minutes or until hot. Serve with shredded iceberg lettuce and each plate topped with a spoonful of reduced-fat soured cream.

30 Grilled Vegetable Salad

Serves 4

200 g (7 oz) button mushrooms
1 red pepper, cut into quarters
1 green pepper, cut into quarters
1 onion, sliced 1 cm (½ inch) thick
2 long green chillies
1 tablespoon olive oil
3 tomatoes, chopped
400 g (13 oz) can chickpeas
2 hard-boiled eggs, chopped
100 g (3½ oz) black olives
salt and pepper

Harissa dressing

1 tablespoon olive oil
3 tablespoons chopped flat-leaf
  parsley
3 tablespoons chopped mint
½ teaspoon ground coriander
½ teaspoon ground cumin
2 tablespoons lemon juice
1 teaspoon harissa

- Preheat the grill. Toss the mushrooms, red and green peppers, onion and chillies with the olive oil and season generously with salt and pepper. Spread out the vegetables on to a large nonstick baking sheet and cook under the grill for 4–5 minutes each side until charred and almost tender, then tip on to a chopping board.

- When the vegetables are cool enough to handle, chop into bite-sized pieces and set aside to cool.

- To make the harissa dressing, mix all the dressing ingredients in a small bowl until well combined and set aside.

- Put the chopped vegetables, tomatoes, drained chickpeas and dressing in a large bowl and toss until well combined. Spoon the salad on to serving plates and top with the chopped egg and black olives.

 Moroccan-Style Vegetable Salad

Finely chop 1 green and 1 red pepper, 1 onion, 2 long green chillies and 3 tomatoes. Mix the chopped vegetables with 2 tablespoons each of olive oil, red wine vinegar, 1 teaspoon harissa and 3 tablespoons each of chopped flat-leaf parsley and mint. Season with salt and pepper and serve topped with 2 chopped hard-boiled eggs, 100 g (3½ oz) black olives with torn pieces of griddled flatbreads on the side.

 Vegetable Skewers with Harissa

Dressing Deseed and chop into bite-sized chunks 1 green and 1 red pepper. Chop 1 onion into bite-sized pieces. Put the peppers and onion in a lage bowl with 200 g (7 oz) button mushrooms, then toss with 2 tablespoons olive oil and season with salt and pepper. Thread the vegetables on to 4 long metal skewers and place on a grill rack. Slide the rack under a preheated grill and

cook the vegetables for 8–10 minutes or until tender and lightly charred, turning frequently. Meanwhile, make the harissa dressing as above. Serve the vegetable skewers with steamed couscous or bulgar wheat, drizzled with the harissa dressing.

30 Lemony Pea Risotto

Serves 4

1½ tablespoons extra virgin rapeseed oil
4 sweet shallots, chopped
1 garlic clove, finely chopped
350 g (11½ oz) risotto rice
125 ml (4 fl oz) dry vermouth
1.2 litres (2 pints) hot vegetable stock
300 g (10 oz) frozen peas, defrosted
finely grated rind of 1 lemon
1½ tablespoons lemon juice
salt and pepper

To serve

finely grated Parmesan cheese (optional)
lemon wedges

- Heat the oil in a large, deep-sided frying pan over a medium-low heat, add the shallots and garlic and cook gently for 4–5 minutes until softened. Add the risotto rice and stir for a minute until the grains are coated in oil.

- Pour the vermouth into the pan with the risotto and simmer rapidly, stirring constantly, until the liquid is absorbed. Reduce the heat slightly and add a small ladleful of the hot vegetable stock, stirring constantly at a gentle simmer, until the stock has been absorbed. Repeat this process until all of the stock has been absorbed and the rice is 'al dente' – about 17 minutes.

- Stir in the peas, lemon rind and juice and season generously with salt and pepper. Stir over the heat until heated through, then remove, cover and set aside to rest for 2–3 minutes.

- Serve sprinkled with grated Parmesan and lemon wedges.

10 Lemony Stir-Fried Rice

Heat 1 tablespoon extra virgin rapeseed oil in a frying pan over a medium heat, then add 4 chopped shallots and cook for 3–4 minutes until softened. Add 300 g (10 oz) defrosted frozen peas, 200 g (7 oz) can sweetcorn, drained, 500 g (1 lb) plain steamed rice and the finely grated rind of 1 lemon. Stir to heat through, then season generously with salt and pepper and spoon into serving bowls. Drizzle with a little lemon juice to serve.

20 Spaghetti with Lemony Pea Pesto

Cook 400 g (13 oz) spaghetti in a large saucepan of lightly salted boiling water for 11 minutes until 'al dente', or according to the packet instructions. Meanwhile, cook 300 g (10 oz) defrosted frozen peas for 2–3 minutes or until just tender in a saucepan of lightly salted boiling water. Drain, reserving 2 tablespoons of the cooking liquid. Tip half of the peas and the reserved cooking liquid into a food processor bowl or blender with 1 tablespoon toasted pine nuts, ½ finely

chopped garlic, the chopped leaves of 1 small bunch of basil, the finely grated rind of 1 lemon and 2 tablespoons lemon juice. Pulse until almost smooth, then season generously with salt and pepper. Drain the pasta and toss with the pea pesto and the remaining cooked peas. Serve immediately.

 # Creamy Stuffed Roast Peppers with Mixed Grains

Serves 4

4 long red peppers, halved lengthwise and deseeded

25 g (1 oz) chopped walnut pieces

500 g (1 lb) ready-to-eat wholesome mixed grains

2 tablespoons lemon juice

2 tablespoons sundried tomato paste

3 tablespoons chopped mixed herbs, such as parsley, tarragon, chives and thyme salt and pepper

Cheese filling

350 g (11½ oz) quark or extra-light cream cheese

3 tablespoons chopped mixed herbs, such as parsley, tarragon, chives and thyme

1 teaspoon grated lemon rind

2 tablespoons toasted mixed seeds

- Preheat the oven to 200°C (400°F), Gas Mark 6.

- To make the cheese filling, mix together all the ingredients in a small bowl and season with salt and pepper.

- Place the peppers on a baking sheet. Spoon the filling into the peppers, then scatter over the walnuts. Cook the stuffed peppers in the oven for 12–15 minutes until tender and the filling is golden.

- Meanwhile, warm the mixed grains in a large pan, or according to the packet instructions. Toss with the lemon juice, tomato paste and mixed herbs and season with salt and pepper.

- Spoon the seasoned mixed grains on to serving plates, arrange the stuffed peppers on top and serve immediately.

Grilled Red Pepper and Cream Cheese Rolls with Mixed Grain Salad Make the cheese filling as above. Spread the filling over 450 g (14½ oz) well-drained, large grilled red peppers halves and roll up tightly. Mix together 500 g (1 lb) cold, ready-to-eat wholesome mixed grains, 2 tablespoons lemon juice, 3 tablespoons chopped mixed herbs as above, 1 tablespoon sun-dried tomato paste and 75 g (3 oz) rocket leaves and serve with pepper rolls.

Creamy Red Pepper Pasta Bake Cook 500 g (1 lb) fresh fusilli in lightly salted boiling water for 3–4 minutes until 'al dente', or according to the packet instructions. Make the cheese filling as above, then beat in 500 g (1 lb) sieved passata. Stir the pasta into the tomato sauce, then scrape the pasta and sauce into an ovenproof dish. Mix 3 tablespoons chopped mixed herbs as above with 75 g (3 oz) fresh breadcrumbs and

scatter over the pasta. Bake in a preheated oven, 200°C (400°F), Gas Mark 6, for 18–20 minutes until crisp and hot.

 # Broccoli and Baby Corn Stir-Fry with Oyster Sauce

Serves 4

2 teaspoons sesame seed oil
2 garlic cloves, thinly sliced
1 tablespoon chopped fresh root ginger
1 red chilli, deseeded and finely chopped
2 spring onions, thickly sliced
1 teaspoon salt
125 g (4 oz) baby corn
300 g (10 oz) purple sprouting broccoli stems
4 tablespoons oyster sauce
2 tablespoons light soy sauce
2 teaspoons toasted sesame seeds

Ginger and lemon grass rice

1 lemon grass stalk
300 g (10 oz) Thai jasmine rice, rinsed 2–3 times
1 tablespoon chopped fresh root ginger
1 teaspoon salt
750 ml (1¼ pints) water

- Make the ginger and lemon grass rice by removing the outer leaves of the lemon grass and finely slice the tender heart. Place in a saucepan with the rice, ginger and salt. Add the measured water and bring to the boil. Reduce the heat, cover the pan with a tight-fitting lid and simmer gently for 14–16 minutes or until the rice is sticky and tender and the water is absorbed. Set aside.

- When you are ready to eat, prepare the stir-fry. Heat the oil in a large wok over a medium heat, then add garlic, ginger, chilli and spring onions and stir-fry for 30 seconds. Add the baby corn and broccoli and stir-fry for 3–4 minutes until almost tender, then stir in the oyster sauce and light soy sauce and simmer gently for 30 seconds.

- Remove the stir-fry from the heat and serve with the ginger and lemon grass rice with the sesame seeds sprinkled over.

 **Chow Mein Stir-Fry** Cook 400 g (13 oz) medium egg noodles in lightly salted boiling water for 3–4 minutes until tender, or according to the packet instructions. Meanwhile, cook the stir-fry, as above. Drain the noodles into a colander, and when the vegetables are tender add to the wok. Pour over 200 g (7 oz) chow mein stir-fry sauce, stir until heated through and serve.

 Stir-Fried Vegetables with Black Bean Sauce Put 300 g (10 oz) Thai jasmine rice, rinsed 2–3 times, in a saucepan with 1 teaspoon salt and 750 ml (1¼ pints) water. Bring to the boil, reduce the heat, cover the pan with a lid and simmer gently for 14–16 minutes or until the rice is sticky and tender and the water is absorbed. Meanwhile, tip a 400 g (13 oz) can of rinsed and drained black beans into a food processor or blender with 1 teaspoon each of finely chopped garlic and finely grated fresh root ginger, 2 tablespoons light soy sauce, 1 tablespoon oyster sauce and 1 teaspoon sugar. Pulse to mix but not to a purée. Stir-fry the vegetables, as above, then stir in the black bean sauce and simmer for 1–2 minutes until heated through. Stir in the rice and serve immediately.

 # Mediterranean Bowl of Giant Couscous

Serves 4

1 vegetable stock cube
150 g (5 oz) giant couscous
250 g (8 oz) mixed cherry tomatoes
175 g (6 oz) drained roasted red peppers, chopped
½ cucumber, deseeded and chopped
1 small bunch of basil leaves
400 g (13 oz) can chickpeas, drained
1 small bunch of flat leaf parsley, chopped
2 spring onions, finely chopped
100 g (3½ oz) reduced-fat feta
salt and pepper

Dressing

50 g (2 oz) roasted red peppes
2 tablespoons lime juice
2 tablespoons aged balsamic syrup
1 teaspoon chipotle or chilli paste
¼ teaspoon garlic purée

- Bring a large saucepan of water to the boil, then stir in the vegetable stock cube. Add the couscous to the pan and cook for 6–8 minutes until 'al dente', or according to the packet instructions. Drain into a large, fine sieve and cool under cold running water.

- Meanwhile, quarter the tomatoes and mix with the peppers, cucumber, basil and chickpeas in a large bowl. Make the dressing by putting all the ingredients in a mini chopper or a small food processor bowl and blending until smooth.

- Mix the cooled couscous with the vegetables and chickpeas, then stir in half of the dressing and toss until all the ingredients are well coated in the dressing. Season with salt and pepper, then divide into serving bowls.

- Mix together the parsley and spring onions, scatter over each bowl of couscous and crumble over the feta. Serve with Mediterranean-style flatbread and the remaining dressing, if liked.

Quick Mediterranean Couscous Salad

Cook, drain and cool 150 g (5 oz) giant couscous as above. Meanwhile, cut 250 g (8 oz) mixed cherry tomatoes into quarters. When the couscous is cold, stir in 2 x 280 g (9 oz) jars mixed antipasti, well-rinsed and drained, and the tomatoes. Toss through 1 shredded small bunch of basil, 1 chopped small bunch of flat leaf parsley and 2 finely chopped spring onions until well combined, season with salt and pepper and serve.

Mediterranean Tomato and Orzo Soup Heat 1 tablespoon olive oil in a large frying pan over a medium heat, add 1 chopped large red onion and 3 finely chopped garlic cloves and cook for 5–6 minutes until softened. Add 250 g (8 oz) quartered mixed cherry tomatoes, 175 g (6 oz) drained and chopped pimiento piquillo or roasted red peppers, the shredded leaves of 1 small bunch of basil, 1 chopped small bunch of flat leaf parsley, 1 litre (1¾ pints) hot vegetable stock and 500 g (1 lb) sieved passata. Bring to the boil, then stir in 200 g (7 oz) orzo. Reduce the heat and simmer for 20 minutes or until the soup is thick and chunky and the orzo tender. Serve with Mediterranean flatbread, if liked.

QuickCook

Healthy Puddings

Recipes listed by cooking by time

3○

Boozy Amaretto Strawberry Meringues	250	Raspberry and Cassis Ice	274	
Apricot and Pistachio Puff Pastry Slices	252	Baked Nectarines with Vanilla and Cointreau	276	
Fresh Berries with Crunchy Oats	254	Mulled Wine Dried Fruit Compote	280	
Sticky Baked Chilli Mango and Pineapple	256			
Lemon Yogurt Cupcakes	258			
Individual Baked Blueberry Flans	260			
Individual Chocolate Pots	262			
Raisin Bread and Butter Pudding	264			
Baked Figs with Dessert Wine Syrup	266			
Baked Spiced Rhubarb with Yogurt	268			
Pancakes with Vanilla Blueberries	270			
Ginger-Marinated Kiwifruit	272			

2○

Individual Baked Strawberry and Lemon Meringues	250
Poached Apricots with Scented Yogurt	252
Quick Frozen Summer Fruit Mini Pavlovas	254
Sweet and Sour Spiced Pineapple and Mango	256
Blueberry and Lemon Sponge Dessert	258
Blueberry Compote Eton Mess	260
Mint Chocolate Dipped Strawberries	262
Cinnamon and Raisin Pear Trifle	264
Figs with Ricotta and Dessert Wine	266
Rhubarb, Orange and Ginger Fool	268
Caramelized Blueberry Topped Pancakes	270
Lime Cheesecake with Kiwifruit and a Ginger Glaze	272

10

 # Individual Baked Strawberry and Lemon Meringues

Serves 4

250 g (8 oz) strawberries, hulled and roughly chopped

1 teaspoon finely grated lemon rind

1–2 teaspoon maple syrup or clear honey, to taste

½ teaspoon vanilla bean paste or extract

2 teaspoons finely chopped mint (optional)

1 large egg white

50 g (2 oz) caster sugar

- Preheat the oven to 200°C (400°F), Gas Mark 6. Put the strawberries, lemon rind, maple syrup, vanilla bean paste and chopped mint in a bowl and toss until all the ingredients are well combined. Spoon the strawberries and any liquid into ramekins or other small, ovenproof dishes.

- Place the egg white in a large, clean bowl and use an electric hand whisk to whisk into firm peaks. Add the sugar, a tablespoon at a time, whisking constantly, until all the sugar has been incorporated.

- Spoon the raw meringue mixture over the fruit in a high peak, then bake in the oven for 5–7 minutes, or until pale golden. Remove from the oven and serve immediately.

 Strawberry, Lemon and Vanilla Cream Tartlets Prepare the strawberry mixture as above. Beat together 1 tablespoon vanilla sugar, 2 tablespoons lemon curd and 200 g (7 oz) fat-free Greek yogurt in a small bowl until well combined and spoon the mixture into 4 small pastry tartlet cases. Arrange the prepared strawberries over the cream and serve immediately.

 Boozy Amaretto Strawberry Meringues Place 450 g (14½ oz) hulled strawberries in a small saucepan with 1 teaspoon finely grated lemon rind, 1–2 teaspoons maple syrup or honey, to taste, ½ teaspoon vanilla extract and 2 tablespoons Amaretto liqueur. Put the pan over a medium heat and warm the ingredients gently for 5–6 minutes or until the strawberries begin to collapse. Spoon the strawberries into 4 ramekins, reserving any excess liquid. Place 1 large egg white in a large, clean bowl and use an electric hand whisk to whisk into firm peaks. Add 50 g (2 oz) caster sugar, a tablespoon at a time, whisking constantly, until all the sugar has been incorporated, then spoon the raw meringue over the strawberries. Bake in a preheated oven, 200°C (400°F), Gas Mark 6, for 5–7 minutes or until pale golden. Serve immediately with the reserved cooking syrup.

1 Poached Apricots with Orange Flower Water and Pistachios

Serves 4

400 g (13 oz) ready-to-eat semi-dried apricots
350 ml (12 fl oz) apple and elderflower juice
2 tablespoons orange flower water
½ teaspoon ground cinnamon
2 tablespoons clear honey
75 g (3 oz) shelled unsalted pistachios, crushed

- Put the apricots in a pan with the apple and elderflower juice, orange flower water, cinnamon and honey and bring to a gentle boil over a medium-high heat. Reduce the heat and simmer for 2–3 minutes until fragrant.

- Pour the apricots and juices into a large bowl and set aside to cool slightly.

- Serve in deep bowl, scattered with the pistachios.

2 Poached Apricots with Scented Yogurt Place 12–16 whole apricots, 500 ml (17 fl oz) water, 350 ml (12 fl oz) apple and elderflower juice, 2 tablespoons orange flower water, 1 teaspoon vanilla bean paste or extract and 2 tablespoons clear honey in a saucepan over a medium-high heat and bring to a gentle boil. Reduce the heat and simmer gently for 10–12 minutes. Meanwhile, beat together 2 teaspoons orange flower water and 150 g (5 oz) fat-free Greek yogurt in a bowl. Spoon the poached apricots into bowls with as much of the cooking liquid as desired. Serve with the scented yogurt and almond thin biscuits.

3 Apricot and Pistachio Puff Pastry Slices Cut a 230 g (7½ oz) sheet of ready-rolled puff pastry into quarters to make 4 rectangles, 14 x 10 cm (5½ x 4 inches). Place the pastry squares on a lightly greased, nonstick baking tray and put 2 drained apricot halves in juice, cut side down, over each pastry section. Mix 2 tablespoons orange flower water, ½ teaspoon ground cinnamon and 2 tablespoons runny honey in a bowl. Brush the mixture over the apricots and put the baking tray in a preheated oven, 200°C (400°F), Gas Mark 6, for 15–18 minutes until the pastry is golden and crisp. Roughly chop 75 g (3 oz) shelled unsalted pistachios, scatter over the apricot slices and serve.

30 Fresh Berries with Crunchy Oats

Serves 4

500 g (1 lb) mixed berries, such as black and redcurrants, blueberries, strawberries, raspberries and blackberries

1 teaspoon orange blossom water

¼ teaspoon mixed spice

1–2 tablespoons soft dark brown sugar (optional)

200 g (7 oz) crunchy oat cereal, such as almond and raisin

- Preheat the oven to 180°C (350°F), Gas Mark 4. Wash and hull the fresh berries, if necessary.

- Place the berries in a large bowl with the orange blossom water, mixed spice and sugar, if using, and toss until well combined. Tip the coated fruits into an ovenproof dish, then sprinkle with the oat cereal over the fruits, pressing down to flatten.

- Bake in the oven for 18–20 minutes until golden and crisp, then remove from the oven and serve immediately.

10 Summer Fruit Compote with Crunchy Oat Topping

Spoon 500 g (1 lb) fat-free Greek yogurt into 4 glass dishes. Top with 500 g (1 lb) puréed compote, such as summer fruits or rhubarb and strawberry, and spoon over 200 g (7 oz) crunchy oat cereal, such as almond and raisin. Serve immediately.

20 Quick Frozen Summer Fruit

Mini Pavlovas Whip 125 ml (4 fl oz) low-fat double or whipping cream to soft peaks and set aside. Put in a blender or food processor 250 g (8 oz) frozen summer fruits, 2 tablespoons clear honey and 100 ml (3½ fl oz) cranberry juice and blend until just smooth but very thick. Spoon the iced fruit mix on to 4 ready-made meringues nests and top each with a large dollop of whipped cream. Drizzle 1 tablespoon blackcurrant or raspberry coulis over each pavlova and serve immediately.

Sweet and Sour Spiced Pineapple and Mango

Serves 4

1 firm, ripe mango

1 small pineapple, sliced in half lengthways and then into thin wedges

2 tablespoons icing sugar, plus extra to serve

Sweet and sour dressing

½ long red chilli, deseeded and finely chopped

4 tablespoons lime juice

2 tablespoons palm sugar or soft light brown sugar

1–2 tablespoons finely shredded mint

- Heat a ridged griddle pan over a medium-high heat.

- Cut 2 sides from the mango, using the stone as a guide and cutting either side of it. Sift icing sugar all over the cut sides of the mango and pineapple so they are well covered.

- Lay the mango, cut side down, and pineapple on the hot pan and griddle for 2 minutes, twisting the pieces once so that a charred criss-cross pattern appears on the fruit. Turn the pineapple wedges over and repeat on the other side. This may need to be done in 2 batches.

- Meanwhile, make the sweet and sour dressing. Put the chilli, lime juice, sugar and mint in a small bowl, then stir until the sugar is dissolved. Set aside.

- Remove the fruits from the griddle pan and arrange on serving plates. Drizzle over the sweet and sour dressing and serve dusted with extra icing sugar, if liked.

 Fruit Skewers with Sweet and Sour Dressing Deseed, peel and cut into rough chunks 1 firm, ripe mango and peel and cut into rough chunks 1 small, ripe pineapple. Hull 12 small strawberries. Thread the fruit pieces on to 8 wooden and arrange on serving plates. Make the sweet and sour dressing as above, then pour the dressing over the chopped fruit. Serve immediately or leave to marinate for an hour before serving, if desired.

 Sticky Baked Chilli Mango and Pineapple Deseed, peel and slice 1 ripe mango and peel and slice 1 small, ripe pineapple. Arrange the fruit pieces over the base of a shallow, nonstick roasting tin. Scatter ½ deseeded and finely chopped long red chilli over the fruit, then sprinkle with 2 tablespoons palm sugar or soft light brown sugar and drizzle over 4 tablespoons lime juice. Put the roasting tin in a preheated oven, 180°C (350°F), Gas Mark 4, for 15–20 minutes until the fruit is tender. Serve immediately, drizzled with the sticky juices and decorated with mint leaves.

30 Lemon Yogurt Cupcakes

Makes 12

100 ml (3½ fl oz) groundnut oil
125 g (4 oz) fat-free plain yogurt
2 eggs, lightly beaten
1 teaspoon finely grated lemon rind
100 g (3½ oz) golden caster sugar
150 g (5 oz) plain flour
50 g (2 oz) ground almonds
1 teaspoon baking powder
½ teaspoon bicarbonate of soda
pinch of salt

- Preheat the oven to 180°C (350°F), Gas Mark 4 and line a 12-cup cupcake or muffin tin with small silicone or paper cake cases.

- Put all the ingredients in a large bowl and beat until smooth, then spoon the batter into the cake cases. Bake the cakes in the oven for 18 minutes or until risen, golden and firm to the touch.

- Remove from the oven and transfer the cupcakes to a wire rack. Serve warm or cold.

 Creamy Lemon Yogurt Mousse

Beat together 1 teaspoon finely grated lemon rind, 300 g (10 oz) fat-free Greek yogurt with honey, 100 g (3½ oz) low-fat cream cheese and 1–2 tablespoons caster sugar, to taste. Spoon the mixture into 4 ramekin dishes and serve sprinkled with 50 g (2 oz) crushed amaretti biscuits.

 Blueberry and Lemon Sponge

Dessert Lay 4 small slices of lemon madeira cake on a chopping board and cut out 4 rounds, about 6 cm (2½ inches) in diameter, to fit inside the bottom of 4 similar-sized ramekins. Place a cake circle in each ramekin and top with 125 g (4 oz) blueberries. Beat together 300 g (10 oz) fat-free Greek yogurt with honey, 1 teaspoon finely grated lemon rind, 2 teaspoons lemon juice and 50 g (2 oz) ground almonds in a bowl. Spoon the mixture over the blueberries, then sprinkle 1 teaspoon golden caster sugar over each one. Place under a preheated grill for 2–3 minutes until the sugar has dissolved. Remove and set aside to cool slightly, then serve.

 # Blueberry and Orange Eton Mess

Serves 4

250 ml (8 fl oz) low-fat fresh chilled custard

200 g (7 oz) fat-free blueberry yogurt

1 teaspoon finely grated orange rind

1 teaspoon vanilla bean paste or extract

150 g (5 oz) blueberries

4 ready-made meringues nests, about 50 g (2 oz) total weight

- Put the custard, yogurt, orange rind and vanilla bean paste or extract in a bowl and stir until well combined.

- Put two-thirds of the blueberries in 4 tall glasses. Spoon over the blueberry yogurt mixture, then top each glass with a lightly crushed meringue. Sprinkle over the remaining blueberries and serve immediately.

 Blueberry Compote Eton Mess

Put 150 g (5 oz) blueberries, the seeds scraped from 1 vanilla pod, 1 teaspoon finely grated orange rind and 2–3 tablespoons freshly squeezed orange juice, to taste, in a small saucepan. Place over a high heat and bring to the boil. Reduce the heat and simmer gently for 5 minutes. Remove from the heat, then pour into a bowl and place the bowl inside a larger bowl filled ice cubes and cold water. Set aside to cool. Meanwhile, whip 150 ml (5 fl oz) low-fat whipping cream, then fold in 4 crushed ready-made meringues, about 50 g (2 oz) total weight. Gently fold half the blueberries into the meringue mix, then spoon into serving dishes. Drizzle the remaining blueberry mixture over the top and serve.

 Individual Baked Blueberry Flans

Spread 4 tablespoons reduced-sugar blueberry jam over 4 individual sponge flan cases. Spoon 150 g (5 oz) blueberries on top of the jam and set aside. Place 1 large egg white in a large, clean bowl and use an electric hand whisk to whisk into firm peaks. Add 50 g (2 oz) vanilla sugar, a tablespoon at a time, whisking constantly, until all the sugar has been incorporated. Whisk in 1 teaspoon finely grated orange rind, then spoon the mixture over the sponge flans and level the surface. Place the flans in a preheated oven, 200°C (400°F), Gas Mark 6, for 5–6 minutes or until starting to turn golden. Remove from the oven and serve immediately with chilled custard, if desired.

30 Individual Chocolate Pots

Serves 4

50 g (2 oz) melted butter, plus extra for greasing
75 g (3 oz) plain flour
1 teaspoon baking powder
1 tablespoon dark cocoa powder
25 g (1 oz) ground almonds
50 g (2 oz) soft dark brown sugar
1 egg, lightly beaten
50 ml (2 fl oz) semi-skimmed milk
125 g (4 oz) raspberries, to serve

- Preheat the oven to 180°C (350°F), Gas Mark 4. Lightly grease 4 mini pudding basins, 175 ml (6 fl oz) each. Sift together the flour, baking powder and cocoa powder into a large bowl. Stir in the ground almonds and sugar.

- Beat the egg with the milk and melted butter in a small bowl, then pour into the dry ingredients and stir until combined.

- Spoon the mixture into the pudding bowls and bake in the oven for 15 minutes, or until risen and firm to the touch.

- Meanwhile, lightly whip the cream to soft peaks.

- Serve the chocolate pots warm with fresh raspberries.

10 Warm Pancakes with Raspberries and Melted Chocolate

Melt 100 g (3½ oz) good-quality dark chocolate in a small bowl over a pan of barely simmering water. Toast 8 mini buttermilk pancakes under a preheated grill for 1–2 minutes, turning once, and place 2 pancakes on each serving plate. Scatter over 250 g (8 oz) fresh raspberries, then drizzle each plate with the melted chocolate. Serve warm, scattered with 2 tablespoons lightly crushed toasted hazelnuts, if desired.

20 Mint Chocolate Dipped Strawberries

Melt 150 g (5 oz) good-quality, mint-flavoured chocolate in a small bowl over a pan of barely simmering water. Completely cover a large chopping board with clingfilm. Dip the tips of 20 large strawberries into the melted chocolate and place on the prepared chopping board. Place in the fridge to chill for 12–15 minutes. Serve when the chocolate has set.

 # Cinnamon and Raisin Pear Trifle

Serves 4

175 g (6 oz) panettone, cut into bite-sized cubes

75 g (3 oz) raisins

1 teaspoon cinnamon

400 g (13 oz) can pears in juice

50 g (2 oz) hazelnuts

500 g (1 lb) low-fat fresh vanilla custard

4 tablespoons half-fat crème fraîche

- Place the panettone in the bottom of 4 glass serving dishes.

- Put the raisins, half of the cinnamon and 100 ml (3½ fl oz) of the juice from the pears in a saucepan over a medium-high heat and bring up to a gentle boil. Reduce the heat and simmer for a minute, then turn off the heat and set aside for 5 minutes.

- Meanwhile, heat a frying pan over a medium heat, put the hazelnuts in the pan and dry-roast until golden. Remove from the pan and crush lightly.

- Beat the custard with the remaining ½ teaspoon cinnamon in a bowl and slice the pears into thick pieces.

- Pour the warm raisin mixture over the panettone cubes and cover with the sliced pears. Pour over the custard and place in the refrigerator for 8–10 minutes.

- Spoon 1 tablespoon of the crème fraîche over each trifle and serve scattered with the crushed toasted hazelnuts.

---

1 Quick Raspberry and Pear Trifle

Cube 4 large slices of Madeira cake and place in the bottom of a large glass bowl. Roughly chop 400 g (13 oz) can pears in juice and add to the glass bowl with 200 g (7 oz) raspberry coulis. Stir all the ingredients gently to just combine. Fold 4 tablespoons half-fat crème fraîche into 500 g (1 lb) low-fat fresh vanilla custard in a bowl, then spoon over the cake and fruit mix. Sprinkle with 2 tablespoons chopped toasted nuts and serve.

3 Raisin Bread and Butter Pudding

Cut 4 large slices of cinnamon and raisin loaf into triangles and layer into 4 large, shallow, lightly buttered ovenproof serving dishes. Scatter over 75 g (3 oz) raisins. Beat 2 large eggs, 175 ml (6 fl oz) skimmed milk, 125 g (4 oz) fat-free Greek yogurt and 3 tablespoons soft light brown sugar in a jug, then pour the mixture over the raisins and bread. Place the dishes in a large roasting tin and add boiling water until the water comes halfway up the sides of the dishes. Bake in a preheated oven, 180°C (350°F), Gas Mark 4, for 20–25 minutes or until the custard is just set. Remove from the oven and serve each dish dusted with 1 teaspoon cinnamon sugar or demerara sugar.

30 Baked Figs with Dessert Wine Syrup

Serves 4

6–8 fresh figs, depending on size, cut in half lengthways
125 ml (4 fl oz) Sauternes dessert wine
2 tablespoons clear honey
pinch of saffron threads
2 tablespoons flaked almonds
4 scoops low-fat vanilla ice cream, to serve (optional)

- Preheat the oven to 180°C (350°F), Gas Mark 4. Lay the figs, cut side down, in a snugly fitting ovenproof dish. Mix together the Sauternes, honey and saffron threads in a jug or bowl and pour over the figs. Put the figs in the oven for 15–18 minutes or until tender.

- Meanwhile, heat a small frying pan over a medium heat, add the flaked almonds and dry-roast until just golden. Tip on to a plate to cool.

- Remove the figs from the oven and leave to cool for 5 minutes before serving. Transfer the figs to serving plates, drizzle with the dessert wine syrup and scatter with the toasted almonds. Add a scoop of vanilla ice cream, if desired, and serve.

 Syrupy Pan-Fried Figs

Cut 6–8 fresh figs, depending on size, in half lengthways. Melt 25 g (1 oz) butter in a large frying pan over a medium heat, and lay the figs, cut side down, in the pan. Increase the heat to high and cook the figs for 2–3 minutes until lightly coloured. Turn over the figs and add 125 ml (4 fl oz) Sauternes dessert wine, 2 tablespoons clear honey and a pinch of saffron threads. Bring to a gentle boil, then reduce the heat and simmer gently for 6–8 minutes or until tender. Cool slightly, then serve the figs with the syrupy liquid drizzled over and scattered with 2 tablespoons toasted flaked almonds.

 Figs with Ricotta and Dessert Wine

Syrup Put 125 ml (4 fl oz) Sauternes dessert wine, 2 tablespoons clear honey and a pinch of saffron threads in a small pan over a medium-high heat and bring to a gentle boil. Reduce the heat and simmer gently for 5–6 minutes to reduce the liquid by about half. Meanwhile, cut 6–8 ripe figs, depending on size, into quarters and arrange in serving dishes. Top each bowl with 1 tablespoon ricotta, drizzle over the warm syrup and serve.

LOW-HEAL-VUE

Quick Spiced Rhubarb and Ginger Fool

Serves 4

150 g (5 oz) fat-free Greek yogurt

150 g (5 oz) low-fat fromage frais

½ teaspoon ground ginger

pinch of ground cinnamon

2 pieces of stem ginger in syrup, finely chopped

2 tablespoons ginger cordial

400 g (13 oz) rhubarb or rhubarb and strawberry compote

125 g (4 oz) amaretti biscuits, lightly crushed

• Beat together the yogurt, fromage frais, ground ginger, cinnamon and stem ginger in a large bowl.

• Stir the ginger cordial into the rhubarb or rhubarb and strawberry compote then, using a large metal spoon, gently fold the compote into the spiced yogurt.

• Spoon half of the mixture into 4 attractive, glass serving dishes and scatter over almost all the crushed amaretti biscuits. Top with the remaining fool mixture, then finish with a scant scattering of biscuits, to decorate. Serve immediately.

 Rhubarb, Orange and Ginger Fool

Place 500 g (1 lb) chopped rhubarb, 4 tablespoons light soft brown sugar, 2 teaspoons finely grated orange rind, 2 tablespoons ginger cordial and 2 finely chopped pieces of stem ginger in syrup in a saucepan. Heat gently over a low heat to dissolve the sugar, then bring up to a gentle simmer and cook the rhubarb for 10 minutes, or until tender. Meanwhile, beat ½ teaspoon ground ginger, a pinch of ground cinnamon and 1 tablespoon stem ginger syrup into 150 g (5 oz) fat-free Greek yogurt and

150 g (5 oz) low-fat fromage frais. Place the cooked rhubarb in a blender and blend until smooth, then spoon into deep bowls topped with the spiced yogurt and fromage frais mixture and 6 crushed ginger nut biscuits.

 Baked Spiced Rhubarb with

Yogurt Place 500 g (1 lb) freshly chopped rhubarb into a bowl with ½ teaspoon ground ginger, a pinch of ground cinnamon, 4 tablespoons soft light brown sugar, 1 teaspoon vanilla bean paste, 1 teaspoon finely grated orange zest and 2 tablespoons ginger cordial. Mix well, tip into an ovenproof dish and place in a preheated oven, 200°C (400°F), Gas Mark 6, for 20–25 minutes, stirring occasionally until the rhubarb is tender. Serve hot with dollops of fat-free Greek yogurt and 8 Italian-style biscotti.

30 Pancakes with Vanilla Blueberries

Serves 4

250 g (8 oz) blueberries
2 tablespoons freshly squeezed
  orange juice
1–2 tablespoons vanilla sugar,
  to taste
vegetable oil, for greasing
4 tablespoons half-fat crème
  fraîche, to serve (optional)

Pancake mix

125 g (4 oz) plain flour
1 egg
300 ml (½ pint) skimmed milk

- Put the pancake ingredients in a blender and process until smooth. Leave to rest for 10 minutes.

- Meanwhile, place the blueberries, orange juice and vanilla sugar, to taste, in a small saucepan over a low heat and warm gently until the blueberries begin to burst. Remove from the heat and set aside to cool slightly.

- Heat a small, nonstick pancake pan or small frying pan over a medium heat and grease the surface lightly with a little vegetable oil. Pour a little batter into the pan and swirl to coat thinly; the mixture should make 8 pancakes in total. Cook gently for 2 minutes or until golden underneath, then flip over the pancake and cook the other side for about 30 seconds. Slide on to a plate, cover with a piece of baking parchment and repeat the process to make the remaining pancakes.

- To serve, fold 2 pancakes on to each warmed serving plate and spoon over the warm vanilla blueberries. Serve with a dollop of half-fat crème fraîche, if desired.

 Quick Vanilla Sugar Blueberry Pancakes Warm 8 ready-made pancakes, according to the packet instructions. Place 2 folded pancakes on each serving plate and sprinkle each plate with 250 g (8 oz) blueberries and 2 teaspoons vanilla sugar. Serve with one-quarter of an orange on each plate, for squeezing over.

 Caramelized Blueberry Topped Pancakes Fold 8 ready-made pancakes into quarters and arrange in an ovenproof dish. Scatter over 250 g (8 oz) blueberries, then drizzle with 6 tablespoons freshly squeezed orange juice. Sprinkle 1–2 tablespoons vanilla sugar, to taste, evenly over the pancakes, then place under a preheated grill for 7–8 minutes until hot and the sugar begins to caramelize. Serve hot with fat-free Greek yogurt.

10 Quick Kiwifruit and Ginger Cheesecake

Serves 4

75 g (3 oz) gingernut biscuits
100 g (3½ oz) reduced-fat cream cheese
75 g (3 oz) low-fat crème fraîche
1 piece of stem ginger, about 15 g (½ oz), chopped
1 tablespoon stem ginger syrup
2 kiwifruit, peeled and sliced

- Put the gingernut biscuits in a plastic bag and crush them using a rolling pin. Sprinkle the crushed biscuits over the bottom of 4 glass serving dishes.

- Beat the cream cheese, crème fraîche, stem ginger and syrup in a bowl, then spoon the mixture over the biscuits. Arrange the kiwifruit on top of the cheesecake and serve.

20 **Lime Cheesecake with Kiwifruit and a Ginger Glaze** Put 75 g (3 oz) gingernut biscuits in a plastic bag and crust them using a rolling pin. Divide the crushed biscuits into 4 tall glasses. Beat together 200 g (7 oz) extra-light cream cheese, 200 g (8 oz) fat-free Greek yogurt, the finely grated rind of 1 lime and 3 tablespoons icing sugar in a bowl, then spoon the mixture over the biscuits. Place the glasses in the fridge for 12–15 minutes. Meanwhile, blend 2 peeled and sliced kiwifruit and 1 chopped piece of stem ginger, about 15 g (½ oz), in a food processor or blender until pulpy but not smooth. Spoon the fruit mix over the cheesecakes and serve.

30 **Ginger-Marinated Kiwifruit** Put 450 ml (¾ pint) apple juice, 1 chopped piece, about 15 g (½ oz) of stem ginger, 2 tablespoons stem ginger syrup and 2 star anise in a saucepan over a medium-high heat and bring up to a gentle boil. Reduce the heat and simmer gently for 8–10 minutes until fragrant. Remove from the heat and set aside to cool. Arrange 4 peeled and sliced kiwifruit and 1 peeled, deseeded and sliced papaya on serving plates, drizzle over the cooled syrup and serve.

Raspberry Yogurt Gratin

Serves 4

400 g (13 oz) raspberries

350 g (11½ oz) fat-free Greek yogurt

1 teaspoon vanilla bean paste or extract

1 tablespoon cassis

2 tablespoons light brown sugar

- Preheat the grill. Place the raspberries in an ovenproof gratin-style dish.

- Beat the yogurt with the vanilla bean paste or extract and cassis in a bowl, then spoon over the raspberries, levelling the surface.

- Sprinkle the brown sugar evenly over the yogurt mixture, then slide under the grill for 5–6 minutes to melt the sugar. Cool slightly then serve.

2 Rasperries, Vanilla-Infused Yogurt and Palmiers
Spread 3 tablespoons raspberry jam over a 375 g (12 oz) sheet of ready-rolled puff pastry. Sprinkle 2 tablespoons brown sugar over the jam, then roll up the 2 shorter sides of the pastry until they meet in the middle. Cut the pastry log into 12 slices and place the pieces on a large, lightly greased, nonstick baking sheet. Place the sheet in a preheated

oven, 200°C (400°F), Gas Mark 6, for 12 minutes or until golden. Remove from the oven and transfer the palmiers to a wire rack to cool. Beat together 350 g (11½ oz) fat-free Greek yogurt, 1 teaspoon vanilla bean paste or extract and 2 tablespoons raspberry jam in a bowl. Spoon the yogurt mix into serving bowls, scatter over 200 g (7 oz) raspberries and serve with the palmiers.

3 Raspberry and Cassis Ice
Place 500 g (1lb) frozen raspberries in a food processor or blender. Add 4 tablespoons cassis, 1 teaspoon vanilla bean extract and just enough raspberry and cranberry juice, about 150 ml (5 fl oz), to blend until smooth. Scrape the purée into a shallow, freezer-proof container and place in the freezer for 25 minutes. Serve with 4 vanilla shortbread fingers, if liked.

LOW-HEAL-XOA

30 Baked Nectarines with Vanilla and Cointreau

Serves 4

50 ml (2 fl oz) Cointreau liqueur
1 teaspoon vanilla bean paste or extract
finely grated rind of ½ orange
2 tablespoons clear honey
4 firm, ripe nectarines, halved and stoned
150 g (5 oz) fat-free Greek yogurt with honey, to serve

- Preheat the oven to 180°C (350°F), Gas Mark 4. Put the Cointreau, vanilla bean paste or extract, orange rind and honey in a bowl and stir until well combined.

- Arrange the nectarines, cut side up, in an ovenproof dish, then drizzle over the Cointreau mixture.

- Put the nectarines in the oven for 18–20 minutes until tender, then remove from the oven and serve with the yogurt, drizzled with any juices from the pan.

 Nectarine, Strawberry and Orange Smoothie
Place 2 x 400 g (13 oz) cans nectarines in juice in a large blender. Add 250 g (8 oz) frozen strawberries, 200 ml (7 fl oz) freshly squeezed orange juice and 1 teaspoon vanilla bean extract. Blend until smooth, adding a little more orange juice if necessary. Serve in tall glasses.

 Nectarines with Vanilla Custard and a Nutty Oat Topping
In a large frying pan over a medium heat dry-roast 50 g (2 oz) fresh breadcrumbs with 50 g (2 oz) rolled oats and 2 tablespoons finely chopped pecan nuts, stirring constantly, until golden and crisp. Remove from the heat and stir in 2 tablespoons golden caster

sugar. Beat together 250 g (8 oz) fat-free Greek yogurt with honey, the finely grated rind of ½ orange, 1 teaspoon vanilla bean extract and 250 g (8 oz) fresh low-fat vanilla custard in a bowl. Stone and slice 4 nectarines and arrange in glass dishes in alternate layers with the custard mix and the crispy oats.

30 Mulled Wine Dried Fruit Compote

Serves 4

300 ml (½ pint) light-bodied red wine

175 ml (6 fl oz) freshly squeezed orange juice

400 g (13 oz) mixed semi-dried fruit, such as raisins, prunes, apricots, dates, pears and apples

½ cinnamon stick

pinch of ground allspice

pinch of ground mace (optional)

1–2 teaspoons orange blossom honey, to taste

1 tablespoon Cointreau or crème de cassis

To serve

4 tablespoons fat-free Greek yogurt

1½ tablespoons toasted flaked almonds (optional)

- Pour the wine and orange juice into a medium-sized saucepan and add dried fruits, cinnamon, allspice, mace, if using, and honey, to taste. Place the pan over a medium-high heat and bring up to a gentle boil. Reduce the heat and simmer very gently for 10–12 minutes, stirring occasionally.

- Tip the compote into a large bowl, stir in the Cointreau or crème de cassis and leave to cool for 10–15 minutes.

- Serve warm with a dollop of fat-free Greek yogurt and a scattering of toasted flaked almonds, if liked.

10 Mulled Wine Smoothie Put 150 ml (5 oz) red wine, 150 ml (¼ pint) orange juice, ½ teaspoon mixed spice and 2 tablespoons honey in a saucepan over a medium-high heat and bring to a gentle boil. Reduce the heat and simmer gently for 2–3 minutes. Put a 400g (13 oz) bag of mixed frozen fruits and 1 banana into a blender, then pour over the hot liquid and blend until smooth. Add extra honey, to taste, then pour into glasses and serve immediately.

20 Mulled Wine Fresh Fruit Compote Pour into a saucepan 300 ml (½ pint) light-bodied red wine and 175 ml (6 fl oz) freshly squeezed orange juice and place over a medium-high heat. Add ½ cinnamon stick, a pinch of ground allspice, a pinch of ground mace (optional), 1–2 teaspoons orange blossom honey, to taste, and 1 tablespoon Cointreau or crème de cassis and bring up to a boil. Reduce the heat and simmer gently for

10–12 minutes until fragrant. Meanwhile, quarter 4 figs, stone and quarter 8 ripe apricots and stone and thickly slice 2 nectarines. Add the prepared fruit with 125 g (4 oz) blueberries to the spiced wine liquid. Bring back to a simmer and cook for 4–5 minutes until the fruits soften. Cool for 8–10 minutes, then serve with a dollop of fat-free Greek yogurt and a scattering of toasted flaked almonds, if liked.

Index
Page references in *italics* indicate photographs

Acknowledgements

Recipes by Jo McAuley
Executive Editor Eleanor Maxfield
Senior Editor Sybella Stephens
Copy Editor Camilla Davis
Art Direction Mark Kan
Design www.gradedesign.com
Photographer Lis Parsons
Home Economist Joy Skipper
Prop Stylist Isabel De Cordova
Production Caroline Alberti